P9-DZN-234

The Rural Life

also by Verlyn Klinkenborg

British Literary Manuscripts

Making Hay

The Last Fine Time

The Rural Life

Verlyn Klinkenborg

Little, Brown and Company

BOSTON NEW YORK LONDON

Copyright © 2003 by Verlyn Klinkenborg

All rights reserved. No part of this book may be reproduced
in any form or by any electronic or mechanical means, including
information storage and retrieval systems, without permission
in writing from the publisher, except by a reviewer who
may quote brief passages in a review.

FIRST EDITION

The Rural Life is a trademark of The New York Times
Company and is used with permission.

Portions of this book originally appeared in the
New York Times and are reprinted with permission.

The wood engravings by Reynolds Stone first appeared in *The Turn
of the Years: The Seasons' Course,* published in 1982 by Michael Russell,
and are reprinted with permission. Engravings copyright © 1982
by The Estate of Reynolds Stone.

Library of Congress Cataloging-in-Publication Data

Klinkenborg, Verlyn.
    The rural life / Verlyn Klinkenborg. — 1st ed.
       p.   cm.
    ISBN 0-316-74167-1
    1. Natural history — United States — Anecdotes. 2. Country
life — United States — Anecdotes. 3. Nature. 4. Klinkenborg, Verlyn.
I. Title.

QH104 .K58 2002
508.73 — dc21   2002141570

10 9 8 7 6 5 4 3 2 1

Book design by Fearn Cutler de Vicq

Printed in the United States of America

The Rural Life is dedicated to my dad,

Ronald Klinkenborg,

who got us all back to the country in the first place

Contents

The Rural Life

January

Every year about now, I feel the need to keep a journal. I recognize in this urge all my worst instincts as a writer. I walk past the blank books — gifts of nothingness — that pile up in bookstores at this season, and I can almost hear their clean white pages begging to be defaced. They evoke in me the amateur, the high school student, the miserable writerly aspirant I once was — a young man who could almost see the ink flowing onto the woven fibers of the blank page like the watering of some eternal garden. It took a long time, a lot of pens, and many blank books before I realized that I write in the

simultaneous expectation that every word I write will live forever and be blotted out instantly.

It's hard to keep a journal under those conditions. It's
harder still when it becomes clear that the purpose of a
journal — at least of those journals begun in earnest on the
first day of January — is not to record, day by day, just a frag-
ment of thought or observation but to herd all one's days, like
so many sheep, into a single pasture and prevent them from
escaping. What drives the impulse toward New Year's journal
keeping is also the shocking realization that the only thing left of
the old year is a few tufts of wool caught in the barbed wire.
What I want a journal to do could be done just as well by a
more aggressive savings program.

A conscientious journal keeper is really the natural historian
of his own life. His model is the amateur naturalists of the eighteenth and nineteenth centuries, writers like Gilbert White or
collectors like George Eliot's Camden Farebrother. It often
seems as though science in this century has little use anymore
for amateur observers of that kind, that science has grown too
institutional, too complex, to value the private watcher of a
small patch of ground. It seems that way too when it comes to
our own lives. They're cross-referenced, indexed, cataloged,
and witnessed by the public and private institutions whose job is
to tabulate and codify us. Even the task of introspection has
been jobbed out to the professionals. A personal journal in our
time comes to seem less like a valuable cache of perceptions
than a naive recitation of symptoms that the writer lacks the
authority to analyze.

January

But many of the great journals — I think especially of Samuel Pepys's seventeenth-century diary and James Boswell's eighteenth-century journal — are not marked by self-consciousness. They're marked by a dogged absence of self-consciousness, a willingness to suspend judgment of the journal itself, if not of its author, in order to keep the enterprise going. The value of Pepys's diary and Boswell's journal is the world they depict and only incidentally the depiction of their authors. Their journals weren't read until long after the authors had died. Both men wrote for an audience of one. Judging by my own fragmentary journals, that's one too many. It's not enough that I should be dead before anyone else reads them. I should be dead before I reread them myself.

So at the beginning of this new year, I'll try to hold out against more journal making. There are lots of good reasons to do so. I have enough to write as it is, and I know enough about writing now to distrust the words that seem to flow onto the page. A journal always conceals vastly more than it reveals. It's a poor substitute for memory, and memory is what I would like to nourish.

But if I do give in, this is what I have in mind. I want to count the crows in the field every afternoon. I want to record the temperatures, high and low, every day and measure the rain and snow. If a flock of turkeys walks into the barnyard, I want to mention the fact. If one of the horses throws a shoe, I want to say so, in writing, before I call the farrier; and I'd like to be able to tell from my journal just how many bales of hay I have squirreled away in the barn. It's no longer the writer in me that

wants to keep a journal. It's the farmer — or rather the son and
nephew and grandson of farmers.

— ◄◆► —

All of the days with eves before them are behind us now for
another year. The grand themes — rebirth and genial carnal-
ity — have come and gone like a chinook wind, bringing a
familiar end-of-year thaw to body and spirit. Now the everyday
returns and with it the ordinary kind of week in which Friday
doesn't turn into Sunday — and Saturday into Sunday — as it
has for two weeks running. It's time for a week in which each
morning throws off a magnetic field all its own, when it's no
trick telling Tuesday from Wednesday just by the sound of the
alarm clock or the mood of your spouse.

With the everyday, winter comes at last to the new year. In
the country it isn't necessarily snowfall or the sudden drop in
temperature that marks the return of winter. It's the sound of the
plow-guy — unless you happen to *be* the plow-guy — clearing
the driveway well after dark, when the dogs are already asleep,
too tired from an afternoon of running around a snowy field to
rise and bark at the scraping and banging outside. In the time it
takes to wonder what the racket is, I remember. It was last winter's sound, and now it's this winter's too. It seems surprising
that the plow-guy even recalls where I live and that such a
flimsy agreement — a couple of words and a nod over a rolled-

down pickup window — could have such presumptive force. But that's the nature of the country, where lifelong service contracts are formed in an instant and attach to the property, not the person, as newcomers discover to their interest. Getting out of those contracts is like getting out of winter. Better just to move.

Winter's own presumptive force made itself plain recently, with rain upon snow followed by snow upon ice late into the darkness. The next morning my footsteps to the barn through the slush the night before had been preserved with remarkable sharpness — each one a life mask of my boot sole, the splash frozen in midair as if it were a Harold Edgerton photo. In the sunshine, snow slid off the metal barn roof with a hiss, and the horses skittered out from the run-in shed, taking pleasure as they always do in a momentary fright. In a single night they've learned how to pick their way over ice again. The roads are suddenly full of the overtentative and the overbold, for at night the cold, clean blacktop looks like hardpacked snow, and sometimes it actually is. Other seasons come abruptly but ask so little when they do. Winter is the only one that has to be relearned.

Somehow it seems appropriate that the year should have ended with a winter storm worth remembering, a walloping northeaster drawing snow down in heaps from a solid ceiling of clouds. This was the kind of storm preceded most richly by anticipation, by the heraldry of radar and rumor, bringing in advance a seasonal glibness to almost everyone in its probable path — everyone, that is, who doesn't have to travel. On Saturday morning the weather drew people to their windows again and again to see how fast the snow was falling, then to see if the fire hydrant had disappeared, then to worry whether the plows were coming. And as always when a storm of this dimension crosses the Northeast, what it brings in greatest abundance is a muffled hush, the sound of nothing doing.

A winter storm is episodic by nature, whether it marches on an arctic track out of the west or rides upward along the coast from the south, as this one did, congealing as it comes. It's been a long time since the last episode of this magnitude, and it was strangely reassuring, if only as a reminder of what true winter really means, since winter is now a pale, warm shadow of its ancestral self. Many seeds require a period of cold, called stratification, before they'll germinate. Thanks to this storm, residents of the Northeast can consider themselves properly stratified.

In the country the storm meant a chance, when the gusts were strongest, to pretend that we'd been shifted northward in latitude to the shores of Baffin Bay, or backward in time to the middle of the last glaciation, when ice sheets rumbled southward across Canada. The snow skidded around the compass with the wind, and though the storm never reached the blizzard conditions forecasters predicted, it was strong enough at times to blot out the dark edge of the forest, to erase stone walls, to

January

weigh down the hemlocks, giving them a more pendulous motion than they usually have. The falling and blowing snow stole color right out of the air, turning a cardinal in a mock-orange bush into an indistinct rose-gray blob. By nightfall the snow in the fields was fox-deep.

⊷ ☰◈☰ ⊶

Every evening just at dusk I carry two hay bales into the middle pasture. One goes into the high feed bunk, the other into the feeder just below it. Each bale is bound by two strings of sisal baling twine. I cut the strings near their knots, which were tied by a mechanical baler sometime late last summer in a Massachusetts hay field. The bale springs apart, and the hay falls into flakes. I coil the strings into a neat loop and put them in my pocket. There's at least one coil of twine in every jacket I own and another in the hip pocket of every pair of jeans. On this place, baling twine is the thread of life.

Not that it gets used for much. It ties down tarps and ties up tomato vines and rose canes. It piles up day by day in an empty grain sack or a cardboard box in the barn. The horses are easier to catch with a double length of twine-string, as my farming cousins called it, than with a proper halter, and the horses are also gentle enough to be led that way. I know ranch hands in Wyoming who never ride out without a loop of the stuff — usually the orange plastic kind — knotted to a saddle-string or a

D-ring. It's hard to describe the emergency that a length of baling twine would fix, but you'd know it if you ever rode into one.

And yet this is the common stuff that gives rural life its substance, a token of what divides this way of living from any other, a reminder of what comes next, what comes every day. Coiling those sisal strands is one of the rewards of doing chores, as is standing among the horses while they crowd together and begin pulling hay from the feeders. The brown horses are mole-dark in their winter coats now, and the dapple-gray mare called Adeline looks ghostly white. Their long hair makes their ears seem especially small, and that makes them all look attentive, though they spend most of the day dozing broadside to the sun's low rays.

If you live with horses, you soon get used to the feel of a line lying across your palm and fingers — a rein, a lead rope, a lariat. It becomes second nature, what hands are for. You begin to feel for the life, the responsiveness in any piece of rope you handle, even a coil of baling twine, because when you work with horses, that line, no matter how stout or supple, is what connects you to them. It transmits the dexterity of your fingers, the guilelessness of your intentions. It becomes a subtle tool. It allows horse and human to moor each other.

Recently the neighbors' horses got out through a broken gate in the middle of the night. They trotted up the yellow line on the highway for a couple of miles, backtracked down a gravel road, and disappeared into the woods. We searched until three A.M., driving the back roads, walking the dirt margins, looking for hoofprints or fresh manure. The night was foggy and there had been no snow. In the end, the horses found us.

January

They walked out of the trees and onto the road we had traced them to. They were wraiths until we haltered them. Then they turned into their old solid selves, a pony, a small mule, and three aging, swaybacked horses, all footsore. And who's to say what we turned into, standing there in the mist, clinging with relief to the lead ropes in our hands? The moon barely glimmered upon us, a knot of creatures on the edge of the winter woods, exhaling together, happy to be connected again.

⚶

Snow has been falling all day long. The skylights are drifted over, and by noon dusk seems to be in the offing, the day so gray, so white, that the winter color of the goldfinches — pale as olive oil — feels like an overdraft on the eyes. Some days chores are barely that, just a visit to the barn and then back for coffee. But this morning the gates were deep in snow and the Dutch doors on the barn needed shoveling out, as did the deck and the path to the woodpile. The horses dropped sweetfeed from their mouths, staining the snow molasses. Three crows in the barnyard stood watch over their shadows, except that there are no shadows on a day like this. One horse had rolled in a drift, leaving what looked like the wingprint of a giant owl descending on its prey.

On the way back to the house, I stopped to clean out the winter entrance to the beehive with my pocketknife. The beehive stands beside a white steppe that will be a vegetable garden one of these days, when April comes and the soil is black and fragrant once more. Yet there's no better day to plan a garden than this one. The landscape has a purity it will lose when the snow melts. The geometry of each bed is perfect at this moment, if hidden.

One mail-order plant catalog is folded open to its pulmonarias. I've dog-eared another where the hostas begin, and in another, from North Carolina, I've marked every plant that could grow in this zone, while lamenting the crinums and kniphofias that won't. *Dirr's Hardy Trees and Shrubs* lies open on the desk beside *The National Arboretum Book of Outstanding Garden Plants*, sources of inspiration and depression. Latin names skim across my thoughts like water boatmen on a summer pond — *Tradescantia, Helleborus, Cryptomeria, Epimedium*. But by afternoon, designs have begun to tangle, and the list of plants is far too long. The only sensible plan I can think of is this one: I'll walk outside with a stick and draw my gardens in the whiteness, echinops here, ligularia over there, a Japanese pieris by this corner. Then I'll sit by the fire while the snow falls, watch them all disappear, and start over again in the morning.

⊷ ⋙⊹⋘ ⊶

Last year it rained all summer. Most of the garden languished, but not the potatoes, which love water. I hilled them twice with compost, and by late August each of the potato beds was a tangle of vegetative sprawl, a mass of deeply dissected leaves and contorted stems. No harvest is quite as satisfying as a good potato harvest. The tubers always come as a surprise, patroon-like and globular in their tight jackets. The vines make a sub-stantial heap, and when harvest is over the ground is suddenly bare and freshly dug, open to almost anything next spring except tomatoes or more potatoes, which might pick up diseases from last year's crop. When I carried the baskets to the house I tried to guess their weight, but the only measure that came to mind was a ton.

I took a potato out of the storage closet this past week and noticed that many of the spuds on the rack had begun to sprout in the cool darkness. On the purple fingerlings there were only small buds, barely noticeable, but on some of the russets and plain white boiling potatoes whose exact variety I can no longer recall, the sprouts had truly begun to rise — about an inch long, pale as potato flesh, already weakly chitted, to use that strange old word.

If the ground had been soft, I could have cut them into sec-tions, an eye apiece, and planted them. And if I had been counting on those potatoes to see me through the winter, the sprouts would have been a dismal sight, a sign that the potatoes would wilt before long and that hunger wasn't far away.

It seems like such an insistent gesture, to throw up sprouts in the darkness of a ventilated closet that once held a small oil fur-nace, with thawed ground so far off in the calendar. Most gar-deners are trying to temper just that insistence in themselves right about now, to honor the heart of winter for not being the shank of spring. I know I'm ready to sprout in the cool mid-winter darkness. Snow is still falling on the garden, blanching the uppermost leaves of the leeks still in the ground. I look at the cherry tree I planted last spring in a corner of the garden and the memory seems very distant.

The ruins of the garden are still just visible above the snow — the tomato cages I forgot to pick up, a single stake from the pea trellis, the bare rose spines, the denuded Japanese maple, and, under the hemlocks, a surprisingly stout spire of *Cimicifuga*. I wake up in the middle of the night and begin to take inventory of the things I plan to do once the snow melts away and the ground begins to soften. Then I remember it's January, a month when only the potatoes are optimistic about warmer weather.

* * *

If deep cold made a sound, it would be the scissoring and gnashing of a skater's blades against hard gray ice, or the screeching the snow sets up when you walk across it in the blue light of afternoon. The sound might be the stamping of feet at bus stops and train stations, or the way the almost perfect clarity of the audible world on an icy day is muted by scarves and mufflers pulled up over the face and around the ears.

But the true sound of deep cold is the sound of the wind. Monday morning, on the streets of Cambridge, Massachusetts, the windchill approached fifty below zero. A stiff northwest wind rocked in the trees and snatched at cars as they idled at the curb. A rough rime had settled over that old-brick city the day before, and now the wind was sanding it smooth. It was cold of Siberian or Antarctic intensity, and I could feel a kind of claustrophobia settling in all over Boston. People went about their errands, only to cut them short instantly, turning backs to the gust and fleeing for cover.

It has been just slightly milder in New York. Furnace repairmen and oil-truck drivers are working on the memory of two hours' sleep. Swans in the smaller reservoirs brood on the ice, and in the swamps that line the railroad tracks in Dutchess County, you can see how the current was moving when the cold snap brought it to a halt. The soil in windblown fields looks — and is — iron hard. It's all a paradox, a cold that feels absolutely rigid but which nonetheless seeps through ill-fitting windows, between clapboards, and along uninsulated pipe chases. People listen superstitiously to the sounds in their heating ducts, to the banging of their radiators, afraid of silence. They turn the keys in their cars with trepidation. It's an old world this cold week.

February

From a distance the woods in winter look monochromatic, gray with undertones of dull red and olive, as if all the trees were a single species. For all I knew, they might have been. Ever since I've lived in the East, I've wandered through a forest of gross generalization, able in summer to tell an oak from a maple and a pine from a birch, but unable to make any finer distinctions. Eucalyptus, manzanita, madrone, juniper, pinyon, even acacia — each of these western trees I recognize, but none of them grows native in the woods around me. What does grow here, I've been able to say rather grandly till now, are trees.

But I awoke recently with a deep taxonomic yearning, an urge to sort the trees in the forest by name. I've found, for instance, that on the east side of the house I live in there are two pignut hickories, enormous, stately trees. Beneath one of them grows a hemlock, a reminder that hemlock is highly tolerant of shade. Until this weekend I had never turned over a hemlock needle and noticed the two white lines that identify it. On the rocky slope north of the house, there are more hemlocks, and compatriot beeches too, elegant, smooth-barked trees surrounded by their juniors, bearing tightly furled buds on the tips of their boughs.

The old barbed-wire fence that surrounds the barnyard was strung along a line of black birches, which grow, the naturalists say, on disturbed ground and which have long since embosomed the wire and staples. Up the hill from an old railroad reservoir, there's a stand of paper birches, on one of which a great sheet of bark has come unpeeled, ready for the presses. Still farther up that hill, in a clearing overgrown with brambles, there's a solitary white pine, whose needles grow five to a bunch.

That's the kind of knowledge you carry into the woods when you first begin classifying — the fundamental keys that allow you to cleave one tree from the mass and call it *Fagus grandifolia* or *Betula papyrifera*. Perplexing as the woods can be at times, there's an underlying order to them. Do the buds on a twig, or the twigs on a bough, grow opposite one another? Then it can't be an oak or a hickory. Do the buds alternate along the twig? Then it can't be a maple or an ash. Spruce needles are square and can be rolled between the fingers. Fir needles are flat and can't be rolled. There's something appealing, especially on a gray winter afternoon, about learning such basic things. Walking through the woods with these keys in hand reminds me of the summer I learned the stars. Night after night I sat up into the early morning, sorting through the constellations and deciphering their movement through the sky. It wasn't enough knowledge to let me navigate the heavens, but it was enough to make me feel at home on Earth.

The Sonoran Desert is greener now than it's been in years. A lush winter like this can almost erase the impression created in other seasons, when the desert looks like a garden of striking specimens set out on a dull, barren plain. Autumn and winter rains have given the desert floor a presence it usually lacks. It's no longer the indiscernible gap, the deserted space between saguaros and ocotillos and chollas, but a level green abundance of its own, flecked with blossom. All its life is now becoming explicit.

The habit in the East Valley of Arizona, outside Phoenix, is to peer into the desert from its edges, to stay on the road — the overcrowded Superstition Freeway and its two-lane continuation, Old West Highway — and look out. From the freeway you can see only how distant the desert edge has become, pushed southward or northward by one housing or retirement development after another. But once you pass Gold Canyon, jumping chollas flicker past at seventy miles an hour, olive-silver, knotted with dangling fruit. On foot the desert edge is deceptive. There's always room for another step, but it doesn't take many before you feel trapped in a fractal maze.

In the towns of the East Valley — especially Mesa and Apache Junction — the major icons of the desert repeat themselves again and again, as they do all across southern Arizona. Old saguaros stand in gravel median strips and xeric yards like crucifixes of loss. Landscapers try wherever they can to re-create the silhouette of the desert, the shadow of heavy-limbed saguaros against jagged mountain profiles. The detail is lost, of course, if only because the astonishing pace of development in the East Valley is a means of imposing simplicity on an unforgivingly complicated and inhuman terrain.

You can find the desert too in the subdivisions and trailer parks and RV resorts that line the roads north and south of the Superstition Freeway, places where Iowans who are fifty-five and older and their counterparts from Minnesota and Saskatchewan convene for the winter. Nearly everyone is here because of the ice at home. They come and go, a bonus army of retired men and women, seeking traction, a foothold. When they want to remember the feel of ice they go to the shuffleboard courts and watch the shuffleboard disks glide back and forth over the waxed lanes, as frictionless as time itself.

Within the walls of these retirement parks, you can hear greater and greater Phoenix, the sirens and the endless rush of traffic. The sound still calls to mind a stiff wind blowing in from the desert. There are ironic allusions to northern lives — an ornamental push-mower bearing the sign RUST IN PEACE, or brightly painted waterbirds welded out of a shovel, a hoe, and the tines of a manure fork. But the desert prevails. Ceramic coyotes and their pups howl silently at the streetlamps all night long. Quizzical ceramic burros ignore their loads and lock you in a sentimental gaze. Ceramic Indian maidens bend low to the water and fill their unfillable ollas.

✦

The premise of the American West has always been that there's another West lying just over the horizon, a place to annul the past, to reoriginate. That premise was never really true, but it was a way of making sense of such a vast quantity of land. Now the next West lies well within the circle of the immediate horizon. East of Denver, heading west, you almost hate to come to a ridgeline on the prairie for fear of what will unfold before you. First a lone outpost of houses clustering on a slope, still raw from the earthmovers' work, then garrison after garrison of signature subdivisions closing in on Denver itself.

For many Coloradans a kind of geographical fatigue has set in, fatigue being another word for a sense of helplessness. The old wounds — the places where a megamall or a new crowd of houses has replaced hay fields and pasture — don't necessarily heal in the minds of some of the drivers inching through Boulder. The shock of the new doesn't necessarily go away when the new turns less new. All around the fringes of Denver, you come across roads like one I took through Lafayette a few weeks ago. On one side of the highway, the old pattern of land use was still visible. Aging farmsteads, mostly shorn of their outlying acres, sat back from the pavement among mature windbreaks. On the other side, the bare earth was glazed with freezing rain falling on a circuit board of newly built houses, already hardwired for an alternate reality.

I often think about some words written a few years before the Ghost Dance massacre at Wounded Knee, more than a century ago, by R. B. Cunninghame Graham, a Scots horseman, essayist, and politician. Graham, who had spent years in Texas, Mexico, and South America, was commenting on the Indian question in the *Daily Graphic*. "The bulk of mankind," he wrote, "declare that a prairie with corn growing on it, and a log house or two with a corrugated iron roof, is a more pleasing sight than the same prairie with a herd of wild horses on it, and the beaver swimming in every creek."

But these scenes — the log house prairie and the wild horse prairie and even those farmsteads near Lafayette — are now so distant in time that they almost seem to be the same place. In America we've learned to locate the meaning of rural life in the past, thereby dismissing it. That's one of the premises behind the sprawl now girdling every city in this nation. Where asphalt-shingled houses spread across the horizon, it sometimes looks like the ash a prairie fire leaves behind. The houses spread almost as fast as prairie fire, but their effect is longer lasting. They are monuments to incomplete arguments, to false assumptions about economic progress and demographic necessity. The strange part is that those endless new streets and new houses almost always enshrine an idea of land use, of community, of living itself, that is already old and failing, an experiment that is tried and found wanting day after day.

The use we make of one kind of land depends on the uses we make of all the other kinds. Denver and environs is the proof. If you turn the Rockies into a playground or, at best, an idealized wilderness, and if you reduce agricultural living to a vestige of an almost forgotten past, then you have successfully cleared the ground for paving the rest of the state clear to Kansas in one direction and to Wyoming in another. To speak from a rural conscience — to say, simply, that this is the wrong way to go about things, a way that's fostered by a deep human venality, a willingness to be bribed into ignorance — is to speak from a place of silence where no one expects to hear wisdom anymore.

***

Just now at home a certain winter weariness sets in. Every morning and evening I can feel the sun pushing back the margins of night. It's a dull soul who hasn't checked sunrise or sunset against his watch several times by now, struck by how early the light comes and how late it begins to go. But that just makes a day of heavy overcast and freezing rain feel all the worse, more of an impairment than it would have been when the sodden year was still shrinking. The rain falls as it has all winter, over ice and snow, as if to make a none-too-subtle point about the climate in this part of New York State, a point that those of us who live here start to take seriously only about now.

The rain falls on frozen ground, and the barnyard looks medieval, a vile compost tea in every puddle. At the bird feeders it looks as though we're running a goldfinch feedlot. Sullen birds shoulder each other aside and seem to squabble more than finches ordinarily do, which is constantly. The other day a mob of robins appeared in the lower pasture on a southeastern slope where the ice cap had retreated. They moved like shorebirds across the frozen turf, staggering forward and falling back, not just that lone bird — the first robin, sign of spring — but a herd, as though there wouldn't be enough assurance in the sight of only one.

I filled the horses' water tank the other morning, and as I did a pileated woodpecker cut across the hillside with a cry of demented hilarity. On dry, cold mornings, the woodpecker goes to work at early light, knocking a row of holes in a hollow tree trunk, waking the woods from hibernation, raising the sap in the sugar maples. The pileated woodpecker forecasts nothing, as far as I can tell. It lives here year round, and its plumage doesn't seem to change, nor does its lunatic cry. Before long, another woodpecker will begin trying to drill through the metal roof of the barn the way it did last year. It will sound as though the world were an empty fifty-five-gallon drum with only the bird on the outside, hammering away. The racket puzzles even the crows in the ash trees.

One day soon the rain will let up, and the frost will leave the ground as stealthily as it came. There will be yielding all around and a sudden insistent adhesion in the barnyard. The urge to clean away winter from the corners of the lawn, from the deep shade beneath the hemlocks, will become irresistible. But all of this hides somewhere on the next page of the calendar. The good news now lies deep within the beehive, where the workers, their dead cast aside into the melting snow, have set the queen laying eggs once again.

March

In the midnineties New England winters had an old-fashioned rigor about them — plenty of snow and temperatures cold enough to make life before central heating look improbable. This winter has lacked that elemental sternness. The bitter weather that stupefied the Plains states largely bypassed New England, which has experienced episodes of balminess. Once or twice the mercury has dipped below zero, and snow has fallen, but to little purpose. What made this winter unusual was ice. In a truly hard winter, ice is something of a scarcity. It appears in all the predictable spots — on rivers, lakes, and ponds — but it's often abraded by wind or covered by drifts. The snowpack in a frigid winter feels almost arid, and moisture is locked up tight. Not so this winter. Days were warm, nights cold, rain almost as likely as snow. Every afternoon the world liquefied a little, and every morning the world was freshly plated in ice.

The roads weren't the problem. Dead level roads are rare in New England. But during January and February, every parking lot or driveway seemed to be a catch basin for the surrounding hillsides, which meant that every parking lot or driveway was a sheet of ice. When the surface of the ice melted in the afternoon, it engulfed the sand that was spread on it the night before. Spreading salt, like tempering steel, only seemed to create a superior grade of ice. All across New England, drivers walked to their vehicles in a gingerly manner, clutching every handhold in sight, only to find themselves stuck on slick, level pavement, often in their own driveways. Some drivers tried to ease off the ice. Some tried to burn rubber right through to the asphalt. In a frictionless universe, nearly everyone would be irascible nearly all of the time.

The ice was beautiful, though it's a beauty most people had had enough of by mid-January. Out in the fields, where the hollows filled with water and froze over, strange vacancies seemed to interrupt the continuity of the landscape. In the rivers, the frazil ice came and went a dozen times. On Dublin Lake, New Hampshire, one arctic morning, I watched a stiff west wind stalemate the closing ice, the whitecaps freezing even as they blew onto a stiffening shelf of frost. And when a light snow fell, just dusting the driveway, it was almost impossible not to admire how slick and unyielding ice can really be. But now the moles are throwing up fresh mounds of dirt. Traction has returned.

⭤

It's been as ugly here as open, undisturbed country ever gets. One day early last week the temperature reached forty-seven in the afternoon, with steady rain. The ground was frozen and still partly covered by snow, which had turned porous and grainy. A dense vapor clung to the tops of the snowbanks. Water ran in thin, scalloped rivulets across tarred roads. It streamed across the earth and pooled in every depression, where it stayed because it had nowhere to go. In every ditch, every hollow, a cold, sepia brew of last year's leaves was steeping in a basin of discolored ice. I found myself staring into the tangled woods, wondering why humans had never learned to hibernate and whether it was too late to think again.

There's a limit to how ugly Manhattan gets in that kind of weather. The light can only fail so far in the rain before buildings begin to glisten. The city never feels quite so immense or so familiar as when the fog closes in. But on a cold, wet night here on the edge of the woods, the opacity is shocking. This isn't the deep sky darkness of December or January, when the emptiness of space seems to reach right down to the horizon. This feels like some suffocating, damp antithesis.

And still, a few days ago the ground was frozen solid. On late October mornings, when the grass suffers a brittle frost, the earth remains soft, though you can feel it tightening underfoot. Now conditions were reversed. In the fields the long grass looked like Ophelia's hair, caught by the current in which she drowned. Yet there was nothing pliant about the earth to which it was rooted. No give at all.

On Thursday, all at once, the soil would take the print of a foot. Not a deep print. As I walked I could feel a thin layer of soil sliding over the frostbound dirt beneath it, like the flesh of the forehead over the skull. By the weekend walking was treacherous, mud over shoes in the wet spots. On drier ground there was suddenly a remarkable sense of leniency. The soil felt almost buoyant, like a gymnast's mat. It invited a fall.

You often hear mud season reviled up here, though no one really misses a bitter winter like this one now passing into memory. In these tentative days at the end of February and the start of March, people talk as though the snow were simply in remission. But when the frost starts to go out of the ground, when even a day with heavy fog holds the light longer than a clear day in late December, I realize that I've thought of winter all along as the still point in the rotation of the seasons. Well, nothing is still any longer. This corner of the planet is melting, and we'll be up to the axles in it any day now.

March

When the snow went away — in a rush, just as it came — it left behind the lawn, the garden, the pastures, the barnyard. It also left behind locust pods, fallen branches, last fall's leaves, snowplow scrapings, mire, and muck — the debris of a disordered season. The snow's erasure has itself been erased. Everything is matted to the earth or anchored in the mud except the ridges an eastern mole has made while tunneling round and round. The early bulbs seem desperate just now. Nothing else catches the hint of spring from them.

Yet the woods look no more disordered than they ever do. Chaos is always thriving just beyond the tree line. Downed limbs wrestle with understory thatch. Birches whose crowns snapped in high wind this winter stand rigid, wounds bright, crowns still waiting for the next high wind to force them all the way to the ground. Somehow that indiscriminate tangle, the mass of all that bare timber, makes spring seem like a betting proposition at best.

I know that there's an underlying order in the woods. What makes it hard to see is its intricacy and its time scale. Any number of interlocking communities dwell in what the eye sums up as a single disarray. All those metabolisms, cross-conspiring, begin to slip out of dormancy about now. The slow fires of decomposition and new growth begin to burn with equal energy. One of the ways to see the order in the woods is to look not at the stands of hemlock or white pine or at the indiscriminate saplings springing up in an abandoned field. The way to see it is to look at the gaps in even the most knotted vegetation. I imagine each of those gaps — the hollow under a bank of snow-matted goldenrod, for instance — as an ecological niche, whose occupants go unseen, who live and die in their own time, unconnected to mine.

That's an optimistic outlook, though it may not sound like it. Gardening at the edge of wildness, I'm able to impose order on nature only so far — a few hundred feet from the house at best. The horses help. They keep the pastures clean-limbed. They like a clear line of sight as much as I do. But in the garden itself — that one word standing in mid-March for a string of murky beds and bare dirt — the purpose is to create a reordering of the wild order, a place of redistributed complexity with an overlying, plainly perceptible simplicity. It will always take imagination to see it at this time of year.

Meanwhile there are all those pods from the honey locust tree. They're lying everywhere, curved, gloss-brown slivers a foot long. People say that cattle love to eat ground-up locust pods. Living in the country you learn to spend money in the meanest ways, and you also learn the most extravagant parsimony. I'm going to rake up all those pods this weekend. I won't be able to burn them or compost them or throw them away. The thought that cattle would eat them will haunt me until I end up getting cattle.

March

To northern gardeners, this time of year is full of anxious pleasure. Even as they daydream about the botanical pleasures of June and July, ordinary mortals find themselves nearly defeated by the gardening deadlines that pass so swiftly in March. Extraordinary mortals — whose seeds arrived two months ago, whose windows are now full of seedlings, and who are ready to sow peas and carrots the instant the soil thaws — will suffer torments of their own when the perfections they're planning somehow fail to germinate or blossom. A garden is just a way of mapping the strengths and limitations of your personality onto the soil. It would be too much to bear if nature didn't temper a gardener's ambition or laziness with her own unsolicited abundance.

March has been oscillating wildly. One day the horses were lying on bare earth in the warm afternoon sun. The next day they stood with their rumps into a wind that was blotting the tree line with horizontal snow. Five inches fell, and again it was possible to follow coyote tracks across a field to a spot where the coyote had dug out a vole. At the edge of a small stream, a weasel had left muddy footprints where it climbed the snowy bank.

This is the season when people with livestock begin counting the bales in the barn, wondering if they can hold out till the pastures green up or the first cutting of hay has been made. Farmers aren't plowing yet, but at six-fifteen on a recent morning, I saw a farmer spreading manure on his cornfields, throwing clods and exhalations of steam into the air behind the tractor. The light had come up early — it's the season for that too — and the very sight of that farmer at work seemed full of hope, a reminder that the soil will thaw, peas and carrots will get sown, and one way or another the garden will grow.

━┿━ ≡◆≡ ┿━

Provident rural residents are already at work preparing next winter's woodpile. Perhaps it's an unwritten rule of the season: stack next winter's wood before you dig this summer's garden. Or perhaps the splitting and stacking of wood is tied to the rising of sap in the sugar maples and the sudden appearance of sap buckets hanging in the woods. There's a keen moral pleasure in knowing that firewood split and stacked and sheltered from the weather in March will burn with abandon in November. Less provident rural residents will buy so-called seasoned wood in September. They'll be plagued all winter long with damp logs and dull fires. When the weather turns sharply colder, their woodpiles will freeze into a single lump.

The lump of firewood beside our house has finally thawed, and an ant — the true harbinger of warm weather — made its way across the bedroom wall and down the page of a book a few days ago. If this time of year is rich in anything, it's rich in expectancy. Everything in nature seems ready to stir, and yet

March

the only thing visibly stirring so far is daylight itself, which is steadily undoing winter. Cold weather has kept the lid on the garden, and the few ambitious shoots that have shown to date seem to be thinking better of it. Ice returns now and then to the small pond in a nearby field. The air looks warm, but it isn't — yet.

What remains most wintry still is the sound of the world at dusk. The chain saws and axes and hydraulic wood splitters stop their work, the traffic dies away, and everything falls silent. A dog barks in the distance, and a white pine creaks. A train rumbles by just beyond the hill to the north, and eventually the last freight car clatters out of earshot. Then, nothing. The nothingness is audible only because it's just about time to listen for the peepers. They'll begin some night before long with a few reedy notes, which will turn, all too swiftly, into uproariousness. Then it won't be possible to remember the quiet of these nights just before the peepers begin. The night sky will suddenly look warmer, more intimate. Orion and Taurus — the winter constellations — will skid into early morning. Humans like to read their own reluctance into the seasons around them. But it's a headlong world in the country, and though most rural residents are provident, not everyone is provident in quite the same way. Some people plan for the winter, and some people plan for the spring.

April

There are 290 bales of hay in the barn loft, enough to last four horses well into the warmth and the tall grass that's coming. Every couple of weeks since late October, I've gone to visit two brothers who raise hay and milk-cows on a Massachusetts hillside. While the brothers stack bales in the pickup, they grouse about the weather and the calamitously low price of hogs and the six-dollar drop in the price per hundredweight of milk. I write a check for the hay — a commodity whose price never seems to fall — and, as part of the deal, I bring news of the weather in other parts of the country — the snow that fell in south Texas in early December, the high winds last month in Lander, Wyoming, the knee-high oats and the peach orchards now blooming in central California.

There's a refrain to these visits. The older brother, who's in his early seventies, compares the actual weather with the predictions published in the *Farmer's Almanac*. The younger brother complains in turn about the inaccuracy of computerized weather reports. I always listen to this singsong with a sense of irony, yet the weather report I want to hear is exactly the kind these old farmers deliver, based as it is on their keen sense of the difference between conditions on their hillside and conditions on ours, seven miles away.

They told me last weekend that the frost is finally out of the earth, all but a crust, that is. They learned this while driving fence posts in a nearby pasture. The woods, they said, are nearly dry enough for the loggers. The brothers recalled that last year they had turned the heifers out onto grass by now and that when the two of them were young boys the oats had to be in the ground by April 15, though they haven't planted that early in a long, long time. This is not the atmospheric science of air masses and isobars and NEXRAD Doppler radar. This is the weather in a world of outdoor labor, weather with a long human memory, where April's drought or flood is still felt in August's hay field, and for many Augusts and Aprils in the mind thereafter. By the time I feed out the hay I stacked last weekend, a year will have passed since it was baled, and my two farmer friends will be baling again.

After I finished stacking hay, I took the chain saw down to a

pile of logs that had been drying in the lower pasture for a full
year, logs that, split and stacked, will dry another summer and
burn next winter. The top logs were warm in the sun, but ice
still clung to the lengths of ash and birch that lay on the bottom.
Snowdrops and aconites had pushed through the brown thatch
near a hickory tree and across the slope to where I sat on a stone
outcrop, resting. It was spring, and it wasn't. The bees droned in
the sunshine, hovering near the lengths of wood I had just finished cutting. In this still early season, the sap that oozed from
the heartwood was the sweetest thing to be found.

⋯ ⋯

If you let a leek winter over in the ground — winter over all
the way till spring — it grows into a monster, a pale, thick-
necked, grasping Medusa. The leaves will have dwindled to a
few dry rasps. They may even have rotted away. But that white-
haired leek head, thrust so obdurately crown downward into
the loam, will not come up without the soil it has entangled over
the winter. Shake it like a chunk of sod to dislodge the dirt,
and the garden fills with white rootlets and the powerful, lingering odor of the leek that would not let go. To eat leeks young is
a kindness to them.

A few leeks remained in the ground from last fall, along with
a clump of unbulbed Florence fennel and a broken row of
carrots, one or two of them firm, the rest top-rotted. I had

forgotten them, and the January frost had heaved them. I dug
them all up. I also dug up hickory nuts and old plant labels. The
garden fork drove tine-deep, and the soft ground was a surprise.
I had planned to do a little probing in the warm spring sunshine, but I ended up turning over the whole of the upper vegetable garden, laying a clod on its side and breaking it up with
the edge of the fork. Soon I was in shirtsleeves, reaching down
to uproot deadnettles, which were already crimson with new
growth. It was an old relationship being worked out all over
again, the perennial weed and the perennial weeder.

Just before the hard freeze in mid-January, we replaced a
200-foot section of post-and-rail fence. The posts had rotted,
but the cedar rails were in good condition. They had turned
gray over the years, and a lichen like the discolorations on a
whale's back had taken root on some of them. This is the sort of
gift that an old farmhouse will sometimes give you — 57 nine-
foot cedar rails that look like something out of a poem by
Robert Frost or James Whitcomb Riley. I laid out raised beds
4½ by 9 feet in the vegetable garden using some of them. At the
moment, the ground is still bare and mounded. It looks as
though I had slain and interred five giants all in a row and not
yet erected the markers. So fearsome is the early gardener.

On Sunday evening the sun seemed to have come to rest
among the birches beyond the pasture. I stood in its prolonged
light and considered the beds. I was impressed by their symme-
try, their intent. Their geometry exposed the rise in that stretch
of the garden, making the land look as if it were bowing to the
southeast. The illusion of mastery was nearly perfect, except

that instead of controlling a deep vertical column of earth, all I had done was to box in the top few inches of the earth's surface. A spade blade's depth beneath the corner of one bed, I knew, there was a rock as big as a subway grate. I could only dream that I'd eradicated the deadnettles.

The earthworms and microbial life-forms commingled as always in the soil beneath the pathways I'd made, making pathways of their own under the rails, dutiful to their own purposes, inattentive to any of my superficial doings except when the garden fork appeared among them. Those creatures are not about to be herded into my corrals.

⊷⊱⊰⊷

"Nor'easter" is a word that people who live in the Nor'east get to use from time to time, as they did on Monday night. Even some of the hill dwellers of western Massachusetts and eastern New York find it hard to say the word without feeling nautical, without imagining that when the wind dies down and the storm settles at last, the yard will be filled with sea wrack and some surprising pelagic debris. But on Tuesday morning the yard was only full of snow and fallen branches — tree wrack. The plows worked the roads all night long, their blades throwing waves of slush into the ditches and striking sparks from the asphalt. Behind them came the tree crews and the power trucks.

The nor'easter was a reminder of how disparate seasonal

cues can be. The eye seems to read the year in one direction, while the ear reads it in another. The tips of the downed limbs in the yard showed the swelling and blush that mark the onset of spring. In the profound, wintry silence of Tuesday morning, the only sound was the distinctly vernal clamor of birds, a pugnacious, whistling crowd of finches, the distant cry of a broadwinged hawk. Red-winged blackbirds crackled to themselves down along the boggy edge of a snow-covered field, creating a strong, almost dizzying sense of temporal dislocation.

A day or two before the storm, the dogs wandered into a neglected garden bed. Its surface was matted with last autumn's leaves, a soggy palette of decomposing browns and near-blacks raised in curious mounds here and there. Beneath the mounds stood new clumps of daffodils, righteously upsprung even under the darkness of six months' mulch. Their spears had been blanched by the lack of light to a pale yellow, nearly the color their blossoms will be when they finally appear. Tuesday morning the daffodils were buried again. Once the snow had been dug away and the sun let in, the warmth of the earth beneath the stems was almost palpable, the soil itself black. That's half the pleasure of a spring nor'easter: knowing that all that snow has fallen on an irresistible season.

April

Let me summarize the situation. Daylight saving time has begun. Snow lies twenty inches deep in the upper vegetable garden, twenty-two inches deep in the lower one. The southern slope of the pasture, bare for a few hours two weeks ago, is covered in snow. Everything is covered in snow except the road, which on good days dries from mulligatawny to gravel chutney. Last week three inches of slush fell — as slush — and it has managed to remain slush ever since. The sun has gone down the woodchuck hole in the high bank by the side of the road and refuses to come out. There's more light at the end of the day now, but that's not where we need it. We need it in the middle.

The signs of spring are thrown away, like unheeded hints. Robins mope in the lower branches of a thick-budded magnolia, waiting for the worms of open turf. The red-winged blackbird I heard in a treetop the other day sounded, somehow, like an asterisk. The chorus of birdsong is entirely different than it was a few weeks ago, but to me it lacks an objective correlative. The tip of a single crocus would do. The house is full of seedlings, especially basil seedlings, all of them at the two-leaf stage, but hooded and mum. The horses are shedding, and it looks like bad management on their part.

I spent a couple of hours moving mud around in the barnyard last weekend, digging shallow channels for the runoff, watching the standing water siphon its way downhill. I pretended to be reclaiming land from the Zuider Zee, opening polder after polder to damp cultivation. It reminded me of a wet spring when I was a boy in Iowa, a spring that filled the railroad ditches and flooded all the low spots in our end of town. As fast as the soil thawed, the flood drained away, washing the ditch grasses flat and releasing a raw scent from the earth, a lowland musk that must have pricked the noses of all the gardeners in town.

When I had drained the last of the barnyard puddles, I threw a hay bale in each of the feeders and went around with the grain bucket. The sweetfeed shone like amber in the dark rubber grain pans. I stood and watched it glowing, suddenly aware of how weary with whiteness my eyes have become, how hungry for color more striking than junco gray. Hunger is the byword for now. On the bare upland stretches south of here, the twilight is crowded with deer. This has been a hard winter for them, and a harder spring so far. They'll be ruddy as the setting sun before long. We'll all be ruddy one day, if that day ever comes.

—▪—⋈♦⋈—▪—

Spring plunges onward, and yet the season seems strangely more patient than it often does here in mid-April. Perhaps it's the long light at evening or the abundance of fair-weather days recently, but a time of year that is emblematic of swift change

April

has offered a consistency, a duration, no one really expects. The grass has risen through old thatch and blossoms have begun to appear on old wood, which reminds you that spring is also a season for dividing the living from the dead — the plants that can't revive, the leaves blown into drifts below the hemlocks, the old stems that won't bud again. Everyone in this neighborhood builds a brush pile about now, and when the conditions look right, they set it afire, as though it were a pyre on which winter burned, the last purification before looking ahead toward summer.

Before we bought it, our house sat empty for several years, so I've been building a Babel of a brush pile at the edge of the woods. Instead of burning it, I'll call it a thicket and turn it over to birds and animals that like heavy cover. What binds the pile together are wild blackberry canes. What gives it body are the burdocks I've been collecting from the pastures. What keeps it from blowing away are honey locust branches too small for firewood. The branches come from a massive bough that fell from the parent tree some years ago, leaving a canoe-sized wound in the trunk. The bough came to rest on a grassy bank that was planted years ago with snowdrops and Siberian squill. It offers a contrast that's almost too easy to moralize — a bough of prehistoric dimension felled by its own weight, while all around it bloom flowers that drove their way up through the snow nearly a month ago.

The locust bough is about eighty years old. I've been disassembling it gradually with a chain saw and axe. One morning I sat down and counted the rings. The wood itself is an umber red, and the rings radiate from the center like dark ripples on a pond. The first time I tried to split a thick, freshly cut cross section of locust, the axe rebounded. When I came back a couple of days later, the disk had developed radial checks — cracks running outward from the center to the bark, across the rings. I tapped the sawn face of one chunk with the back of the axe, and it fell into quarters. Before long, there was a pile of firewood — sharp locust wedges — where there had once been a serpentine log.

But I think I'll leave one length of the downed bough intact, an impromptu garden seat of sorts. The bark is grown over in places with moss and lichen, a patchwork of deep wet green and pale dry olive, grooved and notched and ravined. I've been trying hard, like everyone near here, to bring out my dead during the last few weeks, to rake out the flower beds and borders, to collect the litter of winter. But some days it's been too nice to do anything but sit on an old locust log, still unshaded by the tree above me, wondering about the season ahead, how it will flourish and what it will bear.

I've been thinking about raising pigs. Ask anyone who knows me. Sooner or later the conversation turns to raising pigs. I have a shelf full of books whose titles include the words "pigs" and "successful." I've even sold, as futures, the four quarters of a prospective pig to friends who have decided to humor me. At this moment in Montgomery County, New York, a sow is pregnant, or "in pig," as the pig farmers say, with a litter of piglets from which I hope to take two in May, when they should weigh about forty pounds apiece. The sow and the boar who bred her are Tamworths, an uncommon, endangered breed, lean, gingery bacon types, good foragers, good mothers.

What decided me on pigs was meeting a farmer who still raises pigs on pasture. "I have a pasture," I remember thinking. What all this means is that I'm giving in to the logic of where I live and the land I live on. A place like this is always asking of me, "What can you do yourself?" I didn't even hear the question at first. All I meant to harvest was lettuce and metaphors and peaches in a good year and, of course, bushels of horse manure. But each added layer of complexity — reseeding a pasture or keeping bees — points toward other layers of complexity, like pigs, that lie just a short logical leap away. I have no illusions of attaining self-sufficiency. The only sufficiency I want is a sufficiency of connectedness, the feeling that horses, pigs, bees, pasture, garden, and woods intertwine.

The nineteenth-century English ruralist Richard Jefferies once wrote that "every condition of modern life points in the direction of minute cultivation. Look at all the people in great cities (and small cities, for the matter of that) who cannot grow a single vegetable or a single apple for their own use." I don't know whether Jefferies would have argued that if you can grow vegetables and apples (and pigs, for the matter of that), you should. But he did argue that instead of growing a single crop, like wheat or corn, it might be better for many farmers to grow a wide variety of crops on their land, to cultivate minutely, an idea that has proved true all over the world. The agriculture Jefferies had in mind was a deep biological complexity, not quarter-sections of soybeans.

I'm no farmer, and the land I live on is naturally better suited to growing a little of many crops than to growing a lot of one. The economic argument for raising vegetables and apples and a couple of pigs is small change anyway. But the garden waste and the windfall apples will go to the pigs, as will pasture grasses and hickory nuts and beech mast and some commercial grain. Meanwhile, the pigs will fertilize the pasture and grub out the underbrush at the edge of the woods. In late autumn I'll haul them up the road to a local independent slaughterhouse, which has a smokehouse of its own. I don't know what I will think when that happens, though nearly everyone tries to tell me how it will be.

✦

It's almost impossible to think about nature without thinking about time. In the country, time isn't the fourth dimension, it's the only dimension, and it tugs in an ancestral way that has nothing to do with clocks or calendars. Time in nature is both an axis and a cycle. But it's also a jumble, a collision, especially in the way it works on human feelings. As Milton says of geese,

April

humans are "intelligent of season," and that's a perplexing condition to be in.

Last week, between New Lebanon and Petersburg, New York, Route 22 was an asphalt strip cut right through the natural year. On the highest hills, snow had fallen overnight, clinging to every branch. On the middle slopes, the trees that had begun to blossom looked like plumes of smoke, little different from the smoke that rose from burning leaf piles along the ditches. The Hoosic River had risen to near flooding. In the deepest stretches its waters were thoroughly soiled, but in the shallows they had turned a chalky aquamarine, the color of oxidized siding on a mobile home. In the cornfields, filled with last year's stubble, the first speculative tire tracks had been laid by tractors, which had then turned home because of the damp. Some fields were still covered with an autumnal thatch, while others had sprung so green I almost longed to be put out to pasture.

If the first iris spears and the purple tips of lilac buds still seemed tentative somehow, the birds did not. Robins bombed across the highway only a few feet above its surface. Cardinals took a higher, fluttering path. Turkeys hoping to cross the road collected by twos in the ditches and then departed with a flight that angled steeply upward to end in a distant tree. Crows seemed to hop straight down from the sky to investigate some roadside carnage. From the marshes, I could hear the cackling of red-winged blackbirds. Down among the cattle and horses, which were shedding great strips of winter fur, the cowbirds had returned. The head of a male cowbird is matte chocolate

49

brown, and its body is a deep, night-bright, iridescent black. Trying to stare at the place where those two colors meet evokes a memory that has no name.

Inevitably I search for defining moments at this time of year. Is it the coming of dandelions? The tribe of vultures that gathers in the updrafts? The molting of goldfinches? The hopeful plots of bare dirt — future gardens — newly cut into lawns? In this part of the world each day seems to bring a different, contradictory season. But everything points to the first rhubarb pie.

May

In Manhattan the beauty of the night sky is only a faded metaphor, the shopworn verse of an outdated love song. The stars shine no brighter at midnight in midtown than the ones on the old time-dimmed ceiling of the waiting room at Grand Central Station. But sometimes it's possible, even in Manhattan, to see the evening star — Venus — descending in the west, presenting her orbit, edgewise, to viewers on Earth. Venus is the luminous body hanging low over New Jersey in the early evening, brighter than any heavenly object visible from Earth except the sun and moon. Every night people go to bed wondering what strangely bright star that is, and then they're overtaken by sleep. In the morning no one remembers the question.

Sometimes you can almost picture the motion of Venus in its orbit, as if you were looking at a diagram of the solar system. Imagine a line between the sun, at sunset, and Venus, glittering high above the horizon. That's the line of Venus's orbit. When Venus moves toward Earth, it's the evening star, and when it moves away from Earth, it becomes the morning star. The moment of transition occurs when Venus passes between the sun and Earth. As the year wears on, Venus appears nearer and nearer the sun, until the planet is engulfed by twilight, and then, before long, Venus will come back into view, at dawn. For now, the evening star — Hesperus, as it was anciently known — is a steadily waning crescent, no matter how starlike or globular its light appears.

To say, as you must, that Venus is not a star but a planet seems ungrateful somehow, almost pedantic. That's the kind of technicality Charles Lamb had in mind when defending his personal ignorance almost two hundred years ago. "I guess at Venus," he wrote, "only by her brightness." Lamb was no Copernican, and neither are most of us. We are little Ptolemies every one. The sun rises and sets upon us while the earth remains fixed beneath our feet. When you lie in a meadow, deep in country, late at night, etherized by the fullness of the sky, it's all you can do to imagine the simplest of celestial motions: the pivoting of constellations around the North Star. To impart to each point of light the motions proper to it — to

do the calculus of all those interfering rotations, those intersect-
ing gravities — is simply impossible. It's easier just to imagine
that you're staring at the ceiling of a celestial waiting room.

⊷ ⥤◈⥢ ⊷

Last weekend I woke up at four in the morning to the smell of
rain. Perhaps it was a dream scent. Perhaps a few drops really
fell, enough to remind me that the smell of rain is the catalyzed
smell of the local earth and everything on it. By the time I got
up for good, the ground was as dry as it was when I went to bed,
a month dry, after a month without any precipitation. Dust rises
from the horses' hooves when they run across the pasture.
Manure dries the way it does in Colorado, to half its weight,
then half of that in a day or two. A storm gathered later that
afternoon, portentous clouds, and then, as a neighbor with a
computerized weather station reported, there came nine-
hundredths of an inch, just enough to leaven the upper layer of
dust. We have what might be called a big-gulp rain gauge, and
it registered no such thing.

A spring like this teaches people to see a prescience in
nature, no matter how skeptical they are. All that snow lying so
late into March and April turns out to have been lying there for
a reason, to alleviate this long dry spell. Beneath a dry inch or
two, the soil is still moist. Mud season lasted only a few hours
this year because the melt came so gradually, a sign that the

runoff was being slowly, deeply banked in the soil instead of being sluiced away downstream, down-ditch, down-gully.

The snow disappeared more than a month ago, but I'm still noticing its effects. What remained of the vegetable gardens was mashed flat. In places it looked as if winter had gone through with a stiff brush and a bottle of brilliantine. Winter may have been deep, but it was also soft, and that seems to have suited some species exactly.

The garlic has never grown so well. Nearly every flowering tree and shrub has mocked the memory of other springs with sheer proliferation of blossoms. A week after the snow left, I started seeing tiny seedlings everywhere — in the garden, across the lawn, throughout the pasture. They looked as if they'd been thickly broadcast by someone with a sure hand. Their seed leaves were dark green, but the first true leaves had a metallic glint that gave them away. They were sugar maples. Every samara that fell last year seems to have taken root. We now live in the middle of a forest that's three inches tall. When the sun sets, it catches the tint of the seedling maple leaves and the pasture turns bronze.

━━◆☰◆━━

The oldest cottonwoods along the Bighorn River have fissured bark nearly as deep as my palm is wide, and where cattle have rubbed against them their bark is pale. Morels grow in the new grass beneath the cottonwoods. To hunt for morels is to remember something unsettling about the task of looking. One day last week I searched the partial shade of each tree along a quarter-mile of riverbank, and as I did I tried to concentrate on seeing the fawn-brown cranial effusion that is a morel. But concentrating didn't make the morels appear. They were there or not there, and nothing could induce them to surface where they weren't.

On a bright day a few trout are visible from a high bank — wisps of movement against a dark green background, more angular and better camouflaged than the undulating filaments of aquatic weed that wash downstream. But to some anglers a fish is truly visible only when it rises and feeds. Sometimes trout shoulder the river aside, and sometimes they barely crease it, taking a cluster of midges sliding past on the water's tension, as light as thought. Most of the time the fish adhere to the stream bottom, waiting, feeding in the subsurface drift.

Until the fish rise I wait too. In slack current, rafts of goslings test the water, their parents, like tugboats, nudging them this way and that. Everywhere there is the racket of red-winged and yellow-headed blackbirds, the high-ceilinged squawk of pheasants, the wet slap of mergansers' wings on takeoff. Green hills climb in the distance, level off, and become wheat and barley fields, private inholdings on the Crow Reservation.

Then a morning comes when the wind has died and clouds have hidden the sun at last. The thing that will make the trout appear from nowhere is about to happen. The nymphs of a species of mayfly — *Baetis tricaudatus* — will rise through the water column and hatch on its surface, and the trout will rise with them.

In midafternoon the mayflies are not there, no matter how hard I look, and then a minute later they are. It's as though morels erupted from the grass while I watched, beneath every cottonwood and as far as the eye can see. The mayflies are the same color as the river's dull surface, their wings canted upstream over slender bodies. They drift into view no matter where I look, and coming into view among them are the heads of brown trout and rainbows, suddenly visible at last.

I tried, with friends that night, to estimate how many *Baetis* hatched during the single hour of their emergence. Even the most conservative number looked improbable, and the probable number was unimaginable to us all.

⊷ ≅♦≊ ⊶

It's taken me nearly thirty years — the thirty years since my mother died — to learn that what I miss the most about her is her voice. I can hear it, but I can't tell you much about it beyond what most people know of a mother's voice — that in childhood it fell like consoling shade on a hot ear. So much — the sound of her talking — I missed from the first. More and more, I lack the very way she talked, unadorned and ordinary as it was.

May

My mother's mother said "pie-anna" for "piano." Like her daughter, she sat at that instrument in the intervals of housework and played hymns. Her voice had the reediness that comes to the throat after a hard life. I know a lot about my grandmother, but they're things a child knows, not adult information. I don't know a single sentence her parents ever said to her.

My mom learned in school not to say "pie-anna," and I would wager that she never once used a phrase that was uniquely hers. She spoke, as we all do, a temporal dialect — a speech made up in the main of plain, enduring words, but also of short-lived phrases that belong to a place and a moment. My dad, for instance, knows all the expressions that mark him as a man who has lived through the eighties and nineties. To "go for it" doesn't mean to him what it would have meant to my mom. If I had told her to "go for it," she would have asked what "it" was, where it was usually kept, and why I couldn't get it myself.

Words abide, but new phrases enter the tongue and old phrases exit, reflecting the way the social landscape alters. If, for example, at an old-fashioned family supper, you leaned across the tablecloth to take the yams from under your sister's nose, you were told you had a "boardinghouse reach." It was code for saying, "You're behaving selfishly, like someone who doesn't live in a nice home but has to rent a lonely room and eat with strangers." In short, you got indicted for bad manners, low-class affinities, and antisocial leanings.

You don't hear the phrase much anymore. It evoked a time in the West when laboring men drifted like sand, or a calm dormered establishment with apron-hem rules of behavior against which the strong young men who boarded there were constantly, if coltishly, kicking. These incarnations of the rooming life have disappeared, so we're dropping the expression. When a phrase becomes archaic, as "boardinghouse reach" almost has, an echo from the past vanishes, like coal smoke in an age of gas heat.

Such phrases were only a wrinkle in time, I know, but I miss hearing them anyway. Sometimes I wish I owned a weekend cottage in the country of the old-time tongue — a little cabin near my grandma's lexicon. You could stop by for a touch of Depression wisdom and talk some farm talk. You could stay the whole summer after too much TV. You could come back replenished by speech that summoned the deep past the way the frost heaves stones to the surface of the earth.

Some people believe that the power of the old-time tongue arose from the antique simplicity of living close to the land. Its homey metaphors seemed to spring, like corn, straight up from the ground. Having become a nation of city dwellers and suburbanites, we're tempted to believe that somehow speech is losing its elemental force, that ours is a febrile dialect with twelve synonyms for "rapid transmission of data" and none for "spring thaw." Now and then the grace or wit of a dying phrase strikes home and we remember it. We compare it sadly with our own thoughtless, habitual manner of talking, and the apparent smallness of the modern spirit seems all the more lamentable.

But the power of common speech doesn't grow from the soil or from a simple life or from any other virtue rooted in the past.

May

It stems only from the irrepressible human urge to talk. To find the casual poetry of the past, all you need to do is listen closely to the present. Any day, anywhere, people will say anything. And though I know that all of this is true, I'd like to go back to the past for a time in any case. Not to meet Mr. Abraham Lincoln or to interview the Buddha. I'd like to go to a small Congregational church in Iowa on a Saturday afternoon in May. Outside, my grandfather is mowing the lawn. Inside, my grandmother is practicing the Sunday organ, and my mom is sitting in the front pew with her children, singing to herself the words of the hymn my grandmother, whose name was Nellie, plays. The oldest child pretends to be coloring, but he's really waiting until the mowing and the music stop and his mother and grandparents start to talk together among themselves. He can hardly wait to hear what they'll say.

For the last few evenings it's been almost impossible to come inside before dark. The shadows deepen and converge, the breeze shuffles the leaves in the sugar maples, and an unappraisable sweetness slips down from the woods — all of it with such careful modulation, the entrance of one player after another, that to call it artful sounds like dispraise. I sit and watch from civil twilight until astronomical twilight, from the time the bats first fly, cutting across the bay of light between the trees that line the pasture, until the bats can be seen only when they eclipse the stars.

But no matter how perfect the night is, I always hear a voice in my head saying, "Come inside." I'm not the only one who hears it. I drive along the farm roads, and I can see that everyone else is listening for it too. The dairy cows, freed from their stanchions, drift into udder-deep pastures where they'll spend the night. But the farmers have measured the day out in chores, which are nearly always finished under the glare of a yardlight, whose growing intensity is itself a reminder to go inside. A softball game at a rural school is only a way of postponing the dispersal that will come before long, when the last car door thumps shut in the night and the last driver follows his headlights to the highway.

In small towns the voice saying "Come inside" is painfully insistent. It's written into the architecture, the landscaping, the principled neatness of the walks leading to each and every house. The azaleas bloom with undimmed ferocity even in twilight, and the porches are carpeted in plastic turf and set with plastic lawn chairs. In fading light, unoccupied, they seem to point to the darkness behind the screen door, a darkness broken only by the flickering of a television in another room. There's nearly always a cemetery where the houses end. The streetlamps never light up that part of town. There the good medieval word "curfew" comes to mind, marking the time at night when hearth fires were covered and darkness became absolute.

But on nights as cool and quiet as these have been, why

come inside at all? The temptation is to lie out all night listening to the horses, who stand together, head to tail, in their favorite corner of the pasture. "Rigor now is gone to bed," says the spirit Comus in John Milton's masque, "And Advice with scrupulous head, / Strict Age, and sour Severity, / With their grave saws in slumber lie." Who would choose to join such company? But if you're a mortal reader of Milton, and if you stay outside late enough, you realize that *Comus* is also a poem about the pleasure of coming inside, about fleeing the entanglement of the night, whose otherness feels especially strong the instant you turn for home.

⊰✦⊱

On April 28, the postmistress called. A package had come for me from Claxton, Georgia — four pounds of bees in a wooden crate — and she was keeping it in the bathroom. Late that afternoon, at home, I sprayed the screen sides of the crate with sugar water to quiet the buzzing. I took a nearly empty can of sugar syrup out of the crate and a small cage just large enough to hold the queen bee and a few attendants. I poked a hole in the candy plug blocking the entrance to the queen cage and set the cage in a wooden box called a deep super, the base of a new hive. Then I shook as many bees onto the hive as I could. A few puffs of smoke drove them down into the super. I set a wooden feeder on top, filled it with sugar water, and replaced the cover.

Three weeks have passed since then. The shadbush has bloomed and so have the elderberry and the peaches and the crab apple. The leaves on the trees have nearly all emerged, except for the honey locust, which is always late. I'm late too, still digging garden beds in a patch of soil near the new hive, which sits on a raised platform beside the hive I started last year. Several times a day I take a seat nearby and watch the bees. Workers come steadily, profusely, to the old hive, their legs clubbed with pollen. That hive contains drawn comb — sheets of hexagonal wax cells the bees built last summer — ready now to be filled with eggs, pollen, nectar, and honey.

But when the new bees settled into their hive in late April, all they found was ten framed sheets of plastic, each lightly embossed with a honeycomb pattern. The workers had to release their foreign queen from her cage by eating through the candy plug, a delay that would give them time to adopt her. Some workers began building honeycomb for a bee nursery and larder. Others made foraging flights and repeated trips through the hive to the feeder above them. Bees from the new hive seemed at first to come and go at a different rate than ones from the old hive, and their legs carried less pollen. I wondered every day how they were doing, but it was better to leave them alone.

One warm afternoon this past week, I opened the new hive. A little smoke from the smoker, and the bees scurried down into the frames. I removed the queen cage. It was empty. From the middle of the hive, I lifted a frame covered with fresh comb and in the uncapped cells saw eggs and coiled larvae. The queen was free and laying steadily. Many of the brood cells, where pupae awaited their final transformation into workers, had been capped, turning the wax a soft, rich yellow. In the corners, comb was filled with honey, capped in pure white. There were four such frames, and wax cells were already being raised across the face of a fifth.

The abruptness of spring, its riotous biological opportunism, is always surprising. One day there's bare earth, and the next day the asparagus is four feet tall and ferning out. But there's no surprise quite like that of new comb, new brood, in a new hive, so suddenly there where it wasn't before. Every form replicates itself in this season — every leaf coming true to ancient pattern — but that replication is nowhere as pure as it is in a hive. The comb is perfect geometry, a field of hexagons raised with unimaginable cunning, and the hive is perfect prosperity. The scent of new beeswax drifts downwind to where I sit. Bees plummet onto the entrance board, overweighted with pollen, overburdened with spring.

From solstice till equinox, summer lasts only ninety-one days and six hours, a little longer if you count from Memorial Day till Labor Day. It seems like so much time. But the closer you get, the smaller summer looks, unlike winter, which looks longer and longer the nearer it comes. From a distance — from April, say — summer looks as capacious as hope. This will be the season we lose weight, eat well, work out, raise a garden, learn to kayak, read Proust, paint the house, drive to Glacier, and so on and so on and so on. This will be the season in which time stretches before us like the recesses of space itself, the season in which leisure swells like a slow tomato, until it's round and red and ripe.

By the time Memorial Day comes and goes, flashing across the year like a meteor in the night sky, a certain realism creeps in. The universe expands, but not the calendar. Only August remains infinite. June and part of July are already booked solid, and the trouble with that is that once an event is penciled in it's already over. The festival tickets you bought in April, when summer still had all its weekends, now haunt you with regret. The search for uncommitted time grows more and more desperate. The peonies are nearly past, and before long the goldenrod will bloom. The field-crickets are already ticking away the seconds of full summer.

It's enough to make a person crazy, that dream of a summer where dawn is as cool as the ocean and the time in which you happen to live, the day and hour itself, overlaps with all of the rest of time. Everyone reaches for fullness in summer, but the fullness that most of us know best belongs to the memory of childhood. What was it that made summer days so long back then and made the future seem so distant? What was the thing we knew or didn't know?

May

One of the rules of perspective, which nearly everyone understands intuitively, is that distant objects only appear to be smaller than nearby objects. But imagine a world in which distant objects appear younger than nearby objects, and younger not on the narrow time scale of years or generations, but on an evolutionary time scale. In a world like that you would look at a horse on the distant horizon and see its distant ancestor, running rapidly away from you. The same horse, if it looked your way, would see only the rapidly receding ancestral human in you. This would be a hard world in which to measure time or distance.

Yet that's the universe. Distant galaxies appear younger and less evolved than nearer galaxies because we look at them not only across distance, but also across time. Distant galaxies also appear to be moving more rapidly away from us than nearer ones because, in essence, they still preserve the momentum with which the earlier universe — as young as the light from those remote galaxies — was expanding. Looking out into space, we look into the past, and yet the farther we look, the younger the objects we see. Viewed in this light, "here and now" is the oldest, or rather the least young, place in the universe.

So how old is the universe? A team of scientists led by an astronomer from the Carnegie Observatories in Pasadena, California, has completed a survey of 800 stars called Cepheid Variables, and it indicates that the universe is probably between 12 billion and 13.5 billion years old. These are comforting numbers, if only because they mean that the universe is not younger than the stars within it, a result that earlier estimates had absurdly suggested. But for most of us, these are still problematic numbers. Something about counting in billions makes us dizzy. Previous estimates of the universe's age ranged from 10 billion to 20 billion years. For some reason, this doesn't sound like a very broad range of numbers, though a universe that's 20 billion years old is obviously twice as old as one that's merely 10 billion years old.

Around A.D. 300, Eusebius concluded that the universe was created 5,198 years before the Incarnation of Christ. Even if the universe were only 12 billion years old, it would be 2,182,612 times older than Eusebius thought it was. Somehow that doesn't convey the immensity it should. Neither does the fact that, given these new numbers, the universe is only a little more than three times as old as life on Earth. The difficulty doesn't lie in the age of the universe. It lies in our tendency to imagine all those billions as a single sum and not as the slow progression of one year after another and another and another from the Big Bang till now.

＊＊＊

The dry resonance at night — the ticking of insects — is not as authoritative as it will be in another month. Nor has the city begun to seep with heat, to melt at the crosswalks. Memorial Day is the porch before the house of summer, and spring is still latent here, still discernible in what blooms and hasn't bloomed, in the constellations that haven't yet risen to midsummer's height. If summer is the flat light on a dead-calm sea, the haze that enshrouds the horizon after a week without rain, then this is a time when wind and water are still freshening, still disturbed by echoes from a more vehement season.

It's always striking how holidays that begin as legislative events embed themselves in our sense of the year's natural order. Memorial Day began as a Grand Army proclamation in 1868 to coordinate the decoration of the graves of the Union dead, and it was adopted as an official holiday in 1873 by New York State, the first state to do so. Over time, the holiday, and the decorating of graves with flowers, has embraced the dead from all of America's wars, even as the day itself has lost its commemorative quality for many Americans.

But to anyone who has ever marched in an old-fashioned, small-town Memorial Day parade, there's no forgetting the peculiar stir of feelings that this day brings. It's a morning parade, and it makes its way to a cemetery on the edge of town, a place where cypress grows against the backdrop of clean-shaven lawn and fields of new-sprung corn. An odd moment occurs when the parade arrives at the cemetery. The Boy Scouts and Girl Scouts and the members of the high school marching band look on while their elders, plainly moved though the day is bright and it's not yet noon, honor men — mostly men — who barely figure in the minds of the young people trying to stand at attention. It's always this way, the old honoring those who died young while the young wait impatiently nearby, disbelieving in death.

The Rural Life

To enter summer with an act of solemnity, however slight, however quickly dispelled by the long afternoon that follows the parade, has a certain emotional fitness. It's almost an apology for the thoughtless vitality of this season, a time when the naked exuberance of nature bears the living away into June and July and forgetfulness. Our job now is to live out all those summers that were lost to the men and women who died in wars past, as well as our own summers too. It's no burden to do so.

June

Suddenly the field grasses are knee-high, and in the woods the ferns have completely uncoiled. The first hay has already been cut. A light afternoon breeze now carries the tentative bleating of crickets and the hush of leaves in the trees, sounds that seem to advance the season a month or two. Recently the sun shone for five straight days — a feat virtually unexampled in the past calendar year — and high temperatures reached the seventies. By the third day of steady sun, a cautious delirium had spread among the damp-stained residents of the valley towns nearby. Many persons — especially the old male gossips in village post offices — thought the sunshine was nothing but a sucker play. The root of the New England character is incredulity, a state of chronic, weather-induced heartbreak, and this has been the kind of slow, cold spring in which that character was formed.

For most of May it seemed as though the woods would never give up their bud-red hue or the underlying russet tint of maple flowers. Until a few days ago I could sit on top of a nearby mountain and see on the forest floor the white trunks of birches felled by one of this season's windstorms. The birches looked like the desiccated ribs of some enormous beast whose flesh had melted away in the rain. The thermals rising from the east and west sides of the mountain converged along the ridge, trapping a host of flying insects in turbulence. Swallows pillaged the insect cloud, chattering and diving in raucous motion, the rush of air over their wings almost audible. Not far off, a squadron of vultures slid quietly along the sky, bare heads cocking back and forth, eyes blinking imperturbably. From time to time, a vulture would flap its wings deeply — just once — to correct some imperfection in its otherwise perfect flight.

Now the canopy of leaves has nearly filled in, and when a vulture slips below the horizon, it seems to disappear into the deepening shade that defines the contours of the trees on distant hills. But spring hasn't quite passed into summer yet. In the late afternoon the sun spills through broken clouds onto the expanse of woods that lies west of here, a landscape that rolls outward to the indistinct Catskills. For a moment, caught in that shifting light, the woods shine as bright as a field of mustard.

June

Two kinds of mites have been ravaging bee populations in the United States for the past decade, and my bees are not immune. When you open a healthy hive in midsummer, you can practically feel the frames of honey and brood cells quivering as you lift them, resonating with the pulse of wingbeats and respiration from clustering bees. The enterprise is utterly alive, the collective intact. I took that vitality more for granted than I should have. The bee colonies collapsed, the snows came, and all three hives died. In one of them this spring I found the nest of a mouse that had eaten its way into the sweet darkness and wintered over, unstung. So I began again, but in a different place, and with a renewed commitment to raise bees and let the honey take care of itself. There are two hives now, and on warm days the entrances are choked with bees.

The hives used to stand in the shelter of a stone retaining wall beneath an old elderberry tree. As always, the elderberry budded out in late March, buds as big as bumblebees. Then it stopped, seeming to wait for something that would allow it to flower and bear fruit and draw cedar waxwings into its branches once again. But that something never came. Three weeks ago I backed the tractor up to the tree, looped a chain around its trunk, and pulled ahead. The elderberry popped out of the ground with almost no resistance. But where that dead trunk rose from the earth there's now a stiff green brush of new elderberry stems, two feet tall. They sprang out of nothing, in no time, as if the old trunk had been damming them up. Last weekend I walked down to that corner of the garden and tried to comprehend that those bright stems are the same plant as that gnarled old tree. I can't quite grasp it.

For some reason the sight of that elderberry carried me back a year, to a hospice room in Sacramento where my stepmother, Sally, whom I'd known for more than half my life, lay in a coma, dying. All life support had ceased, and those of us who gathered around knew that the self within her had withdrawn for good. But the vigorous breathing continued, one day, then another and another. I can still feel the force of those breaths, the elemental power of the reflex that drove them. The conscious life we live seems so fragile that it comes as a shock to witness the organic thrust toward living that underlies it. I never understood the optimism or the power of that reflex until I watched, hour after hour, the raw persistence of those unthinking breaths, which finally ceased while my brother John and I stood over her one night. Our breathing seemed shallow by comparison.

Sometimes it seems as though I grew up in the backseat of the family car, face plastered to the window. Summer after summer we drove from Iowa to the Black Hills, to Wyoming, to Colorado, never eastward. We also lived a hundred miles, in oppo-

June

site directions, from both sets of my grandparents, whom we visited again and again. The car hummed along the high asphalt crown between the ditches. We drove through thickets of grove shade and farm scent. Barnyards gaped suddenly as we passed and then they closed again as quickly.

The way to look at it all was to accept its passing. To see something interesting you had to be looking right at it as it flew by. If you didn't see it, you wouldn't see it, no matter how quickly you turned your head or how hard you looked back down the road. There was no entanglement with the scenery. Sometimes a farmer would wave from the field or a woman from beside a rural mailbox. Sometimes a driver coming the other way would raise a couple of fingers. That was it. In the far distance the horizon slowly revolved while houses and outbuildings, cattle and soybeans, seemed to fling themselves past us along the roadside, slowing only as we came to the outskirts of a town. A lot of us grew up that way.

But in this present life, I sometimes ride an old quarter horse named Remedy up the gravel road that runs past our place. The pace of travel is different, of course, and the scenery is no longer self-contained. A drama taking place in a driveway or a side yard doesn't elapse in a split second, as it does when you drive by in a car. It has a chance to play out, and our passing changes the way it plays. As we ride along the road, Remedy and I are always trading measures of alertness. He notices everything long before I do, but he's surprised by things I happen to know are not surprising. We're implicated in the world. Everyone waves, and we wave too. People come out onto their porches and pull curtains aside to look, and we look back. There's more than enough time for acknowledgment.

East of our place runs a two-lane blacktop road just like the ones that crisscross Iowa. Most of the time it's pretty quiet, but for a few hours on weekends it carries a lot of traffic. Squads of bikers come rumbling down the hill, while RVs struggle up the hill. On Saturdays a parade of pickup trucks towing race cars makes its way to the track ten miles northwest of us. In winter and on rainy days, truckers rattle their jake brakes all the way down the hill.

Whenever I work in the vegetable garden or attend to the bees or feed the horses, I step into an amphitheater that rises from the road. I imagine myself as a child driving past in the backseat of the family car, looking across a pasture at a man walking down the yard in a bee suit and a veil. I'm visible for only a second and then I'm gone.

⊶ ⩥◆⩤ ⊷

A visit to Walden Pond doesn't resolve the image of Henry Thoreau. What it does instead is clarify the contradictions, the disparities from which that image is shaped. The light rising from the surface of the pond on a June afternoon reflects indiscriminately on the objects around it. The same was true of Thoreau's mind, no matter how ill assorted the objects he wrote about might have been. What harmony there is in Thoreau's thinking, I believe, came from the collision of dissimilar ideas, the struggle, as he might have put it, between the acorn and the chestnut obeying their own laws.

Thoreau's best work is the result of two very different but complementary perspectives. One came about when he refused to pay his poll tax and was jailed in Concord for a night. Of the village and its institutions on that evening, he wrote that he was "fairly inside of it." The other perspective was, of course, the one he took when he chose to live fairly outside of Concord, in a small, handbuilt cabin on a rise above Walden Pond.

Both stances, for that's what they were, were honored a couple of summers ago in a clearing on Pine Hill, just southeast of the pond, by a crowd that included the president and the first lady. The occasion was the dedication of the Thoreau Institute and the permanent conservation of ninety-six acres of the Walden Woods, both brought about by Don Henley, lead vocalist of the Eagles.

President and Mrs. Clinton had come to Walden at Henley's invitation. So too had the professors who introduced Henley to Thoreau's writings, and so had Mohandas Gandhi's great-granddaughter and Ed Begley Jr. and the rest of the Eagles. And so, most improbably of all, had Tony Bennett, who jogged out of the Walden Woods and onto the stage as if it were the Copacabana. He sang one unaccompanied verse of "America" and then trotted back into the arms of the waiting foliage. It was an afternoon of disparities, which the bright sun did nothing to dispel.

When the president stepped up to the lectern and leaned his

arms across the top, I couldn't help thinking of what Thoreau noticed during his night in jail — not the striking of the town clock or "the evening sounds of the village," but the fact that he'd never "seen its institutions before." I'd never seen the institution of the presidency in person before, but the man on the stage stood deep within it, and he talked about the distortion it created, remembering a time when he and his wife could walk in the woods without the experience seeming more real to observers than it did to the two of them.

It was a basic trope of Thoreau's mind to search for a point of view slightly higher than the one you could gain from the top of Pine Hill. He couldn't say what you might see from the very highest vantage point, but perhaps his own was high enough. "It is not many moments," he wrote, "that I live under a government, even in this world." I tried to imagine what Thoreau might have said about the tribute being paid to him from so deep within a primary institution of a government he barely acknowledged, but there were too many answers, all of them true and all contradictory.

⊷ ⪥⬦⪤ ⊶

When the early bird sings at four A.M., the only other sound is the dogs running out their dreams at the foot of the bed. Somewhere on the Atlantic the sun is already rising, but at our place the sky at that hour is no brighter than tarnished silver, a supe-

76

rior dullness in the eastern windows. The early bird is extremely early, and it seems to have perched on the bedside lamp, so piercing is its call. In the phonetic language birders use to represent birdsong, the early bird says, "Why don't — you get — up? — Why don't — you get — up?" But at four A.M. it's all too easy to drift back to sleep. Soon the early bird seems to be saying, in dreamlike fashion, "Guess what — you've just — won! Guess what — you've just — won!" It's worth putting on some clothes and going to find out.

It's forty-four degrees outside. The grass is wet with dew. Breath hangs in the air almost as quietly as Venus in the southern sky. The early bird, a nesting robin by the sound of it, is stationed in the boughs of a pine across the road. The clarity of the robin's call is a measure of the silence. It will be a windy day, the trees full of their own noises by afternoon, but for now their stillness enlarges the scale on which this solo bird performs. When the robin pauses for a moment, I can hear everything in the world, because there's almost nothing to hear.

Winter mornings hinge on just a change in light without much change in sound. But a summer morning when the sky first glows is a cathedral of anticipation. The choirs that Shakespeare had in mind are neither bare nor ruined, only silent, until one by one, and then all in a rush, the birds fill in. It was never quite so clear before this morning's walk that song is an attribute of light. The birds understand it perfectly. A finch begins to call in a lazy, staccato pulse, the rhythm of an inexpert seamstress on an old-fashioned Singer. A cardinal starts to spear the air with his voice. Down at the foot of the grape arbor, a cowbird suddenly fizzes and pops. The canopy of trees is answered by the understory, and the tall grasses in the eastern field fill with birdsong too. One by one the birds add depth to the horizon, until at last there's room for the sun to rise.

⊷ ⩺◆⩤ ⊶

It's been an abrupt, sodden spring in southwestern Montana. The rivers are full of snowmelt and will be full for many days to come. At Carter's Bridge, just south of Livingston, the Yellowstone River sucks at the concrete pilings with a low, hydraulic hiss. The discolored current swarms with floating debris, mostly cottonwood branches, their bark half stripped by the commotion. Upstream and down, the river gnaws at its banks, pulling away great fragments of earth, which struggle for a moment and then succumb, dissolving in a darker swirl of water.

In Yellowstone National Park, not far from the western entrance, there's an enormous meadow where, in normal times, the Madison River bends away from the road toward a cliff face in the distance. Last week that meadow was totally submerged. I stood near the road and watched bison wading belly-deep across a limitless sheet of water, as if they were amphibious. They moved somnolently, all except one young male who was running to catch up with the herd, splashing his way in the bright sunlight. He looked like an American version of the bull who carried Europa out to sea. Some bison had

78

managed to climb up onto the roadway. They swung their heads as they walked, their fur hanging in tatters, like seaweed, from their flanks.

Still farther into the park, along the Firehole River, the buffalo wallows had turned into tide pools. In some there was only a dense swirl of algae, but others quivered with temporary life, the nymphs of aquatic insects trying to conceal themselves from a burning sun. Here the bison were dry, their sleek, red calves grazing beside them. When they're this young, buffalo calves look like they belong to a different species than their parents, who seem to be all head and spine. The difference in appearance causes much confusion. One visitor, watching an early June herd of adults and young, asked a local angler which were the buffalo and which were the bison. A truly perplexed tourist praised the Park Service for assigning St. Bernard dogs to guard the herds.

Slowly the bison on the Firehole River drifted out of the hot sun and into the timber. They left behind a carcass of their own kind, now many days old and still pungent. A solitary raven did a questioning dance across the river, its ratcheting call echoing over the water. In the far distance, an angler walked down to the murky flow of the Firehole. With his rod beneath one arm, he lifted his hands together, apparently to pray. He stood that way for a very long time. He was selecting a trout fly, as if, under such unpromising conditions, his choice might actually make a difference.

The Rural Life

The dogs hear it in the distance before I do, and so do the horses, a dry dislocated thump, thunder from far away. One moment there's no wind, the air still and damp. The next moment the wind is turning corners where there aren't any, lifting and coiling the barnyard dust. Wind flails the leaves on the sugar maples, revealing their silver undersides. It scatters spent hickory flowers in drifts. The sky blackens, and I can almost hear rain begin. But then the wind drops and the front unravels over the western ridge, where the weather comes from. Blue sky intervenes. A clear night threatens once again, Venus hanging peaceful in the dusk.

It's gone on this way for several days here in the midst of a dry season. Rain promises, and then the cloud cover, which was as tight and dense as a peony bud, blows away in loose tatters to the east. There's no point waiting for thunder to crowd in overhead and rain to fall. But a single thump sets everyone listening, ready to count the seconds between the flash and the crack of the storm, ready to welcome the hard downpour if it ever comes, though it will cut the garden soil and beat the last of the peonies to the grass.

And yet somehow the need for rain domesticates the very idea of a thunderstorm. Were a storm to blow in now, soaking the earth, it wouldn't be Wagner that ushered the thunder across the treetops and into the clearings, tearing at tree limbs and driving the horses into a frenzy. It would be Rameau, and in the beat of the thunder coming overland there would be something folkish and formal at once, a country dance welling up through the refined strains of an operatic suite.

The horses would circle the pasture in a ground-eating trot, and the trees would sway in some sort of unison, a hiss arising from the new rain on their leaves. I'd hear the clatter of the downpour on the barn's metal roof all the way from the covered porch. The Shakespearean undergrowth on this small farm — the dame's rocket and cow vetch and ground ivy — would twitch under the heavy drops, and the old question of how bees fly in rain would present itself once again.

Only then would something come unhinged in the music of the storm, the lightning moving too close, the shade deepening too abruptly, one of the dogs fetching his breath up short with anxiety. The cataclysm would gradually slide across the valley, and as it did Rameau's music would be heard again, dying away in the east, the ground sated with rain. If only the storm would begin.

Iowa farmers used to call a stalk of corn growing in a soybean field a "volunteer." I've always loved the personification lurking in that use of the word, as though a cornstalk among the soybeans were like a zealous schoolgirl sitting in the first row of desks, arm thrust in the air after every question. Farmers get rid of volunteers with chemicals now, but in the early 1960s they organized gangs of kids to walk through the bean fields pulling up volunteers as well as the real weeds. This was called walking, or cleaning, beans. The goal, of course, was higher yields, but there was also a German vanity lurking in the desire for a perfectly clean field and perhaps also a perfectly disciplined child.

This place is choked with volunteers, nearly all of them welcome. In fact, if the plant community on this place consisted only of individuals I had put in the ground myself, or that had spread from seed of my sowing, it would resemble one of those fading Midwestern farm towns where the schools have closed, the grocery stores have pulled out, and the only new building in town is the nursing home. Instead this place is crowded with life. Outside my second-story office window, the leaves of a birch tree living in a planter tap against the screen. I had nothing to do with it. Potato vines claw their way out of the compost heap, no matter how often I turn it. On the north edge of the vegetable garden, a young hickory has started up out of nowhere, but in exactly the right spot.

Last summer I planted a striped-bark maple called *Acer tegmentosum*, which came all the way from California. A few days ago I took a walk up the dry creek bed behind the barn, a ravine that thunders with runoff after heavy rains, looking for the spot where its water goes underground. I noticed a familiar leaf and realized that I was surrounded by a grove of striped-bark maples — a species called *Acer pensylvanicum*, but otherwise almost identical to the one in the garden.

Walking back to the barn, I crossed a slope filled with maidenhair ferns, not a bit different from the cultivated one we put beside the hostas last spring. The hillside, once a field, had filled with saplings. A couple of years ago, you might have mowed them down with a bush hog. No longer. They've passed the point where they could accurately be called volunteers. Now they've made the place their own.

＋－ ≋◊≋ ＋－

In 1969 my father and I drove from Sacramento, California, to George, Iowa, to gather a few of my grandmother's belongings. She had lived at the edge of George in a house of dark wood-work, scented by geraniums standing in the winter windows and by a slightly scorched odor from an old electric stove. When my grandfather died, much of the substance seemed to go out of that house, and my grandmother followed him into the earth soon after. Now all that was left were empty cupboards and closets and drawers. We took home to California a stiff wooden chair and an old rolltop desk that had stood in a small room on the second floor, its drawers stuffed with valueless yen brought back by one of my uncles from the postwar occupation of Japan.

For most of their adult lives, my grandparents lived and worked on a farm northwest of George. My father grew up there, and it was unclear what he felt when we came to visit it, as we often did when we still lived in Iowa. I still feel a kinship to that farm — to the house and grove and a long-since reordered pattern of fields — without ever pretending that my feelings could serve as a sort of levy on the place. I suspect my father felt the same way. There wasn't enough land in the family for every one of his father's children to inherit a farm of their own. Besides, this was America, the Midwest, where the idea of a legacy in land only a couple of generations under the plow seemed almost czarist. Instead of farming, my father became a public-school music teacher, a career that appeared to lead away from the soil. In 1966, when he was thirty-nine, he moved west from Iowa with his young family and started again, as many Iowans did, in California.

A few years later Dad bought thirteen acres in the oak and madrone hills east of Sacramento, within sight of the Sierra Nevada, and my brothers and sisters and I came home for part of the summer of 1978 to help build a house there. The foundation slab — a rectangular pool of concrete that looked like slick water on an overcast day — had already been poured when I arrived from New York. It was notched into an eastern slope overlooking a ryegrass pasture studded with ponderosa pines. And that's where an old conversation with my father resumed — how expansive that slab seemed, how perfectly level, how smoothly finished, and what it promised about the house we would build upon it with our own hands. Plumb and level and square — while we worked our talk realigned itself around those perfectly unambiguous standards. As subjects go, plumb and level and square sound too rectilinear, but not in the mouths of a father and son looking for something to say. "Close enough" — both of us eyeing a spirit level laid against a beam or along a header — became words of genuine, unexpected complicity.

June

There had been years of do-it-yourself construction in our household, years of work with drill and hammer, shovel and saw, day after day when I might have spoken this particular language with my dad. When I was a young boy he taught me how to nail together beehive frames and brood boxes in the basement of our house, which he and his brother-in-law built. There was always a project of some kind under way — turning a garage into a bedroom, pouring a new patch of concrete, reroofing the house. But by the time we moved to Sacramento and I entered high school, I was already living on some dark planet orbiting between my ears, inaccessible to the humble claims of amateur carpentry. And no wonder. When Dad got up from the dinner table, disgusted beyond words with another of my ironic impieties, he usually retreated to the woodshop he had built near an apricot tree in the far backyard. Silence and glum looks fell all around the table whenever that happened — until from the shop, rising high above the sounds of traffic on Watt Avenue, came the repeated, inarticulate scream of a table saw. I used to joke that Dad was crosscutting two-by-fours and pretending that each piece of pine was my stiff, impenitent neck. Only my mother found it hard to laugh.

One after another these images gather — crossing the high plains of Wyoming more than thirty years ago during the long drive "back," as we always said, to Iowa, both of us watching the moonlight on the snow between Rawlins and Laramie — the two of us wandering, not quite together, through my grandmother's empty house in George that bitter cold Easter — the sullen distance between us as I drifted into private insurrection

85

in high school and college — and then a picture of him standing between the studs of a wall we had just raised on that new foundation, while behind him, well off to the east, rose the granite peaks of the Sierra Nevada, all their difficulty smoothed by distance.

Now, so many years later, I find myself in a new relation to the old story. I'm as old as my father was when the shape my young life was taking must have looked most hopeless to him, when he might have given up guessing altogether the shape my life would take. Lindy and I have no children, and when the state of our childlessness occurs to me, as it often does, I also think of something my brother John said when his son, Jake, was born — that he suddenly understood Dad in an entirely new way. Instead of a child to understand my father by, I have an old house and this land — a pasture, stone walls, outcroppings of bedrock, and ordinary, acidic soil set in a largely graceless climate. Every time I walk out onto this property with a tool or a pair of gloves or a purpose, I think of my dad walking out, in exactly the same manner, onto his property in the foothills of California. I realize that I've been caught up in an urge — an atavism really — that reaches well past the limits of my own nature. I've discovered a stirring, restless desire to improve this place — to father myself upon it.

My plan in buying this small farm wasn't to tutor the pasture and the sugar maples and the hemlocks. I hoped instead to let the landscape tutor me, to lie fallow for a while myself. But most days I find myself walking out the mudroom door in old jeans and a torn jacket and leather gloves. There are asparagus crowns to be trenched or apple trees or roses to be planted or a garden plot to be tilled. An entire pasture needs refencing. The chain saw needs sharpening, and when that's done there's a pile of logs to be cut into stove lengths. One of the yard hydrants leaks, and the barn needs to be emptied, cleaned, redivided, rewired, hay stacked, manure hauled.

Some days I do just the one thing that needs doing most, whatever it happens to be that day. But many mornings I leave the house and find myself, hours later, in a trance of physical labor, covered in sawdust or mud or sweat, muttering quietly to myself. This is the very work I hated as a kid, the thing I dreaded whenever my dad came into a room where I sat reading. "I need some help," he would say and then walk out the door ahead of me, a little slumped in the shoulder, perhaps from knowing how grudging my help would be. It's not grudging now. I used to believe you could choose your influences. That's the principle behind every rebellion. Now I know that they choose you.

A few years ago I learned that my dad had consulted seriously with his father before moving to California in 1966. It was a small detail, but it reminded me that his life was not just an adjunct of my own. When I was young, he had always been in the public eye, even if it was only a small-town public. He was a bandleader — the man who stood at the conductor's podium in the high school gym, who directed summer concerts in the town park band shell, whose white, gold-braided band uniform hung stiffly in the closet. I had watched him playing cards with his wry farming brothers, their wit more caustic than his own, with a gift for irony that he has never had. I had seen his perennial optimism — his self-assurance. I noticed how readily people turned to him for practical advice and how sound that advice usually was. He tended to exaggerate, and he had a hard time admitting the limits of what he knew, but whenever I noticed those things he was in the presence of his smart-ass kid. From time to time, when I was still a boy, he took me outside town to visit farmers he knew — men whose children he had taught to play clarinet or drums. Those farms awoke a different man in him, the same one I saw working in the woodshop or garden. I was so bent on avoiding that work when I was young that I never wondered how my dad had learned to do it or what part it might have played in an inner life that was truly his own.

Until he left home for college in 1943, my dad followed his dad into the predawn darkness in work clothes every morning, headed for the dairy barn or the machine shed, a map of the day and its connection to other days already in my grandfather's mind. I barely remember seeing my grandfather at work on the farm, only an image of watching him turn in the seat of an old Farmall tractor while shelling corn in late autumn or winter. The farm, when I first knew it, was still very much what he had made it over the years, though he lived in town by then. But when he and I drove out to the farm from town, I felt acutely that I was coming as a visitor and that my grandfather was arriving himself in visitor's clothing. His familiarity with the families, most of them relatives, who lived behind the windbreaks on the horizon, his keen appraisal of the crops in the fields and the condition of the cattle and hogs, the intimacy with which he knew the farmland itself — that was simply lost on me.

But "intimacy" is probably not a word my grandfather would have used to describe the way he knew his land. Intimacy implies too equal a balance between farmer and farm and not enough subjection of the soil. It's also too private a word. There's something public about the open terrain of northwest Iowa, something public too about the progressive way my grandfather farmed, as well as the role he took in George, a town his own father, who emigrated from Germany at eighteen in 1884, had helped found. What my grandfather really possessed was an intimate acquaintance with the character of his own labor, a private, unspoken awareness of how far he could push himself, how strong he was, where he was weak, and what work gave him greatest satisfaction. The intimacy with which he knew his land was really a reflection of the intimacy with which he knew himself. Both kinds of knowledge were tempered by self-expectation rooted in a roundly public sense of community whose social topography was defined by close kinship, the presence of so much family, so many Klinkenborgs. All these things were fostered, in one way or another, in his children.

When I returned to California in 1978 to help my parents raise the frame of their new house, I saw that for the first time in my life, and perhaps in his life too, my dad had found a scale of living — a landscape for his labor — that matched the scale of self-expectation he had seen in his father. Dad no longer owned just a house and yard, but a place we began, half-joking, to call the ranch. Working at the building site that summer, every one of us knew that some inner tension in the family had been released, a prospect enlarged, a dead end narrowly averted. In 1966, when we arrived from Iowa, Sacramento was a rough, unreconnoitered city only apparently gentled by the presence of so many government offices. By the time my parents moved to the edge of the mountains a dozen years later, a paralytic blandness had settled over the city and its cul-de-sac suburbs, a blandness as palling as the tule fogs that blind the San Joaquin Valley every winter. But on thirteen acres high above the fog, under a canopy of ponderosa pines along the Georgetown Divide, my father rebuilt a warm-weather version of his childhood, complete with cattle, sheep, hogs, chickens, tractors, and the obligation to walk out onto the land in his work clothes — a short-sleeved shirt and a pair of grease- or pitch-stained pants — every day when he was done with school. And by rebuilding his childhood he reframed the rest of my adulthood.

If I counted all the days I spent working beside my father at the ranch over the past twenty-five years, they would total only three or four months. And if I tried to make a list of the things he taught me directly in that time, it would be a short one. There wasn't much to teach in most of the work we did together in those years. Burning a brush pile doesn't have many fine points. And, as we both learned long ago, my father and I are ill suited as teacher and student. He's impatient to move on to the next job, because he has a long list of jobs to finish before lunch, and I'm impatient because I know that some expert has written a book or an article about whatever we're doing which I can read at leisure. But every time I came home, something new had sprung up — an automated irrigation system, an apartment above the barn, a carport, a gazebo, new roof, new paint. The number of animals rose and fell and rose again. And soon, enough time had passed for decay to set in, for the first fences we built there to look run-down, like relics of a forgotten California. All the things Dad intended to do on the ranch began to coexist in an almost melancholy way with all the things he actually did.

When you take on a property like the one my parents bought — thirteen rolling acres divided by a narrow irrigation ditch, broken by veins of rock, and covered in poison oak and head-high Scotch broom — you simply set out to clear the land and find a building site. But you leave traces of yourself with every decision you make, every fence you build, every tree you fell or plant, every quarter-acre you choose to irrigate or leave dry. In twenty years' time, a self-portrait emerges, and it exposes all the subtleties of your character, whether you like it or not. The land and the shape of the buildings show precisely how much disorder you can tolerate, how many corners you tend to cut, how much you think you can hide from yourself. Neatness may reflect nothing more than a passion for neatness, or it may be a sign of small ambitions. And beyond the literal landscape — the one that has been tilled and planted or logged or fenced or simply let alone — there is the ideal landscape that lives only in the mind. Every day you explore the difference between the two, knowing that you can see what no one else can.

At the ranch I could walk in a minute or two from the lightest, most orderly region of my father's personality — the woodshop or the apple orchard — across the irrigation ditch and down to a subliminal clutter of welding rods and oilcans and greasy tractor parts in the dark precincts of the barn. In a corner near the highway lay a part of the property my dad almost never visited, a dry, dusty tangle of raspberry brambles that must have pained him whenever he passed it on his way to the mailbox. Just a hundred yards off lay a grassy, well-watered ridge where he must have looked up from his work sometimes and marveled, as I did, at what he had made of this property. If you drove in the upper driveway, you came to a rose garden and a well-kept lawn. If you took the lower driveway, you found fuel tanks standing by a dilapidated corral, grass growing through the frame of an old sawmill, a sun-blistered camper shell resting on blocks. But I never once came to visit without seeing in those things the profusion and self-confidence of my father's character. I hope the mess I make speaks as well of me someday.

Dad is now seventy-six, healthy, vigorous, almost adolescent again, as seventy-six-year-olds tend to be these days. A couple of years ago, just before my stepmother's health failed, my parents sold the ranch and moved back down the mountain to a new development on the outskirts of Sacramento. They bought a house not one stick of which they put up themselves, and my dad started saying what a relief it was to have so little yard work to do. Now that I have a small farm of my own, I almost believe him. Still, my dad added a screen porch to the new house himself. He planted tomatoes where his neighbors might have hired a gardener to plant camellias.

It had never occurred to me that the ranch would be sold while my parents were alive. I felt the way I did when I learned that my grandmother's house in Iowa was being put up for sale, the way I'll feel if the home farm near George ever leaves the family. Every day I miss the ranch, not for its beauty alone, but because it was so inexpressibly of the people who made it. It was home to a part of me I didn't know existed until the summer we built the house there. That June, my brother John and I camped out on the foundation, lying awake late at night to watch the stars overhead. My arms were tight from hammering all day long, my back brown. The thought that in a few weeks I would return to the East Coast and a life among books and letters — a life purely of my own choosing — was inadmissible. Some of Dad's friends came to work on the house with us, and I was surprised to discover that my impatience with their ineptitude was more than matched by my father's impatience with them too. It was the first sign in years of how much we had in common, or rather it was the first sign I was willing to accept.

This farm of mine — these few bony acres — is the estate I've inherited from my father, a landscape both tangible and intangible. That's how I think of it. It's a way of propagating what I've learned about him and myself. It carries me back to a time when I was very young, standing at the edge of the garden in a small Iowa town watching him work a hive of bees. He wore white coveralls, a helmet and veil, and he stood on a stepladder because the hive was so tall, the honey flow from the surrounding farm fields so heavy. When Dad was here last June, one of the first things we did was walk down to look at the bee-hives on the edge of the garden. Then we worked together for a couple of days building a run-in shed for the horses. But as we set posts and measured rafters, I realized that I wanted to be building *his* run-in shed, not mine. I wanted to be adding another structure to a property he no longer owned, assuring a continuity of man and landscape that would last another thirty or forty years. I knew then that I would have to go on with this work alone, that someday it would have to be both father and son to me.

July

At first light, about four o'clock, the bats begin fluttering at the roof ridge, slipping into the house through a bat-stained crack between clapboards. It's just enough noise to wake me up, and for a moment I lie there, watching the dark shapes against the false dawn outside. The bats nest somewhere in the ceiling above my head, just beyond a layer of Sheetrock and insulation. It's like having a chicken coop in the rafters.

It's pleasant to pretend that wildness stops at the front door in the country, but it really doesn't. In April I started seeds under a lamp in the basement, and when the seedlings were just ready to be pricked out and potted on, the mice grazed them down to bare stubs one night. A fox took a seat in the driveway the other morning and looked at the kitchen as if he expected to come in.

At night flying insects clatter and whir against the screen of a lighted window, and sometimes the bats pick them off the screen, their wings just brushing it as they fly past. It comes as a surprise to realize once again how full the night is with insects. Moths come flaring into the headlights like stones skipped down the highway. Last week I walked down to the mailbox long after dark. Out in the open, where the darkness lessened, I saw an atmosphere full of insects drifting past, like the metropolitan scene in a science fiction movie, airborne traffic vectoring this way and that. Twice in the past week I found the corpse of a luna moth on the ground. It seemed less like the remains of a personal moth death than the wreck of a pale green, iridescent, freight-carrying kite. As full as the air is of insects, it is that full of insect eaters too.

But as far as I can tell, no one's eating the slugs. We try not to. We wash the lettuce from the garden three or four times, picking over each leaf carefully before we spin it dry. The profusion of slugs this year reflects the damp, dark weather that has clung since April. Slugs are a kind of animate precipitation, aqueous sloths. The garden is flecked with them in early morning, and after I've tossed a few of them into the nettle patch, the revulsion they cause dies away — until one turns up on the salad plate.

What we're missing here, in this kingdom of airborne bugs,

July

is barn swallows. I don't know where they are. The barn is ready and waiting. There are open pastures, and there are horses. There's an overhead wire to perch on and gape at the world from. We don't spray, and we don't knock down swallow nests. So where are the birds? Phoebes take bugs on the wing, and so do the few tree swallows who live around here, and of course the bats. But it isn't the same. Some quality about this place, some aspect of its rusticity, won't be official until the barn swallows move in.

On the Fourth of July, the instinct is always to look backward in time, to the first news of that great Declaration, or to the days when Emerson could truly say that "the vast majority of the people of this country live by the land, and carry its quality in their manners and opinions." That habit of looking backward is a little like taking a rowboat under the pier once a year to see for ourselves that the pilings are still sound. It restores our confidence. It also reminds us how many transfigurations this nation has gone through over time and assures us that through all those changes there is a discernible continuity of political purpose, the same vested interest in independence. We still carry the scale of this land in our manners and opinions, if no longer the actual touch of its soil. We carry something, too, that our ancestors couldn't: the scale of our own history.

One of the things you notice while looking backward on the Fourth of July is that everyone you come upon is looking forward. "It is the country of the Future," Emerson said in 1844. Anyone else you might turn to, anyone else who has taken up a pen on the subject of America, says something similar. What Emerson meant, in part, was that his generation, as well as the young men he was speaking to, had devoted themselves to creating institutions whose benefit would be realized when they were long gone. "We plant trees," Emerson wrote, "we build stone houses, we redeem the waste, we make prospective laws, we found colleges and hospitals, for remote generations. We should be mortified to learn that the little benefit we chanced in our own persons to receive was the utmost they would yield." Emerson's future was not an abstraction. It lay in the institutional and social and physical landscape around him.

Looking back, you come again and again upon a jubilee of prose, a feast of optimism, an unparalleled faith that nature itself will redeem the American enterprise. That's the Emersonian strain in our history. But alongside that strain you can always hear the question that Crèvecoeur asked in his *Letters from an American Farmer* in 1782: "What is an American?" Men and women have given a lot of thought to that question, trying to puzzle out how the influences that shaped this nation would weigh out. The question hasn't changed in all this time, though the influences have. A country born in a sense of limitlessness has found its natural, geographical limits. That day was always bound to come.

July

In a way, those early generations of Americans were unable to think of themselves as the future someone else had intended. Some were present at the revolutionary rupture with the past, and others, who were not, helped articulate its moral and political implications, which still felt as fresh to them as last night's rain. But we must think of ourselves as the future someone else intended, because we are. Every eighteenth- or nineteenth-century attempt to suggest the potential of American liberty is a prediction of sorts. Some of them are sober and some wild beyond belief. But we're living in the shade of those trees, in those stone houses, and under the aegis of those prospective laws. It's still the country of the Future, but it's also now the country of a rich, embracing Past.

⊷ ≡◈≡ ⊶

The Fourth of July steals over a small town daydreaming the summer away. A young boy rides his bicycle in a serpentine pattern down the middle of a dusty street. Blue sky divides a broken pavement of clouds. The road out of town seems to stretch farther than usual before it fades out of sight between fields of corn or soybeans, alfalfa or cotton. Near a railroad siding, the silence of noon is broken by the sound of a mechanic's hammer ringing against steel in the darkness of a repair shop. An old horse sleeps in a small corral behind the drive-in. The mail fails to arrive. A firecracker goes off in the alley.

99

It's hard to believe that such towns still exist. Harder still to realize how many of them there are, once you leave behind the cities and the suburbs and the unincorporated sprawl and break out into the open. But in those towns the Fourth seems to come into its own, whether it's a hamlet like Texas, Ohio, little more than a bait shop on the north bank of the Maumee River, or a place like Lander, Wyoming, where the Fourth goes off like the crack of doom.

The Fourth has no precise rituals. Some families serve potato salad at their picnics — those who have picnics — and some serve coleslaw. The bunting comes out of mothballs, and the high school band — in some disarray now that the seniors have graduated — prepares to march down Main Street playing Sousa. If the town is small enough, the parade will turn around and go back the way it came.

The self-reliance of small towns is easily mistaken for complacency, and the casualness of the Fourth in such places can be misread as indifference. The Declaration of Independence isn't read aloud, nor is the Gettysburg Address. But when dusk comes and fireflies and crickets begin to go off under the trees, the park fills with people who have walked the few blocks from home for the fireworks. Grandeur isn't on the program, nor is exaltation, just some modest municipal detonations, some rockets that rise shrieking over the fairground or river, worrying every dog in town. The sound of pale thunder breaks right overhead, and for once the lightning lasts long enough to see, raining earthward in a shower of sparks.

July

Since the first Fourth, Independence Day has been celebrated in just about every possible way, with emotions ranging from a throb of sanctity to irate mockery, with fireworks, parades, doubleheaders, hot dogs, speeches, demonstrations, and long afternoon naps on what feels delightfully like the second Saturday in the week. This is still the least commercial holiday in the American holiday roster. No one has figured out a way to sell the public on exchanging Independence Day presents, and you can only use so much red, white, and blue bunting before the front porch and the eaves start to look overdressed. The few things that always sell well for the Fourth — explosives — are illegal in most states. One good flag lasts a very long time.

In some celebrations of the Fourth — not many — there still exists an attractive vein of rationalism, a recognition that what's being celebrated is both an event and an idea. Rationalism doesn't sound like a very patriotic emotion, or much like an emotion at all, but it's the spirit in which the Declaration of Independence was written, and it reflects a historic part of the American character, a brusque, native skepticism that's rarely honored enough these days. In the phrasing of the document, in the way it was promulgated, there was an assurance that reason was preferable to sentiment and that the reason embodied in the Declaration of Independence would be sufficient to dissolve whatever feeling still bound Americans in that era to England.

You hear it said repeatedly that the Fourth is America's birthday, which is true, but not true enough. The emotion the holiday most often summons is patriotism, love of country, which is good, but not good enough. A rodeo queen in sequins races into the arena in a western town, circling the crowd on a fast horse, standing in her stirrups, the American flag she holds snapping in the wind while the announcer lets his voice overflow with feeling. Everyone in the grandstand rises and their hearts rise too, mostly. This is a fine thing, but it's not what has carried us all these years, not this alone, no matter what form it takes.

By now it's almost impossible to read the words of the Declaration of Independence — especially its unequivocal statement of self-evident truths — without emotion, without acknowledging, at least, that its rhythms ring with a familiarity next door to emotion. But the Declaration doesn't adjure its signers or the people they represented to strong feeling or, for that matter, to patriotism. It adjures them to a sober consideration of causes and first principles based on the laws of nature. It speaks not only to the idealism of its first audience but also to its pragmatism, its sense of justice. These are the qualities that have preserved the fundamental idea with which this country began. We speak as though conviction were always an emotion and as though emotion were the deepest experience a human could know. The authors of our freedom knew better.

July

A mosquito lies on its back, dead, on a sheet of white paper on a desk. Its banded legs are thinner than script from the nib of any pen, and they point straight toward the ceiling. Under a magnifying lens the mosquito — a female — resolves into a hairy thoracic ball, delicately fringed wings, a segmented, countershaded abdomen (dark above, light below), a pair of antennae, some mouthparts called palps, and eyes that seem to focus, cross-eyed, on the tip of its needlelike proboscis. She looks like what she is: a drilling rig with wings. She died from effrontery. She floated down through the lamplight and into full sight on the inner arm of the human who killed her. He was able to watch the mosquito deliberate as she stalked slowly into position. When her legs stiffened and he imagined he could hear the hydraulic whine of the drill about to bore into flesh, he struck. Without anger, without vengeance, but not without pleasure.

Insects tap and flutter against the window, borne in through the darkness on a tide of light — mayflies and caddis, moths and beetles, pulled off course by the glow from a reading lamp. Out in the night itself, fireflies have nearly reached their summer's peak. Where the lawn ends and the field begins, a wall of vegetation has grown up, thicker and for its height more impenetrable than any rain forest on earth. Above the grass heads and seedpods and leaves and fronds, the fireflies stutter like slow sparks. They constellate and then, for a moment, they all go dark at once.

Mosquitoes never blink to each other, nor do they flock to a lit pane on the side of a house. They are not so easily diverted. Before converging on a victim, they seem to pause, to create the illusion that this one summer evening will be biteless. It must be quite a sight to see a human through skeeter eyes. There he stands, hatless, barefoot, in T-shirt and shorts, an incandescent pillar, a beacon of warm blood at the edge of the field. On his face there's a slow-footed look. He thought he would just walk down to the field to watch the fireflies for a minute. He thought the night would be empty except for the bugs he could actually see in the dark. But the night is not empty. He swats at the shrill pitch in his ear and gets bit behind the knee. He bends to rub it and gets bit on the ankle. He scrapes his shoulder against his neck and slaps at his arms. He thinks he can stay ahead of the bites, but he is always behind. Each prick on his skin is already farewell. He pretends to saunter up the lawn to the house, as if nonchalance mattered to the mosquitoes drifting in upon him. He stoops once more, stops sauntering, and starts to run.

———— ❧ ————

A couple of years ago, judging by roadside signs, it looked as though the rural economy of America depended almost entirely on the sale and resale of Beanie Babies. On every country road you passed hand-lettered squares of cardboard, nailed to a fence or tied to a mailbox, announcing the availability of

July

Beanie Babies. If you didn't know what Beanie Babies were, the signs could be confusing — LAMBS FOR SALE at one farmstead, PIGLETS at another down the road, and BEANIE BABIES at a third. As I drove home from the train station the other night over an hour of country roads, I realized I hadn't seen a BEANIE BABIES sign in a long time. That sector of the rural economy has moved to the Internet.

But the roadside is still a public market. Never mind the farm stands, which are now coming into their midsummer glory. What I mean is the person who builds utility trailers, one by one, in the garage in his spare time and then parks them beside the road with a FOR SALE sign on the hitch. Or the kids who run a summer business selling small bags of CAMP WOOD by the side of the road for about $1,000 a cord. Nearly every farm has a lot, usually behind a machine shed, full of old implements half-buried in tall grass. Some of them are genuine antiques, some are too good to be given up, and some are junk. But every now and then there is one that is just the right vintage — a 1980s feed wagon, say — to be stationed out near the ditch. You don't even have to see the FOR SALE sign to know the wagon is for sale. Something about its position says it all. The wagon isn't really talking to the weekenders heading upcountry. It's talking to the farmers who drive by it every day, for whom the blacktop highway is still a local farm road.

There's a gesture in those roadside offers — the short red school bus, the $1,100 pickup — that I can't help admiring. At first they look like pure dismissal, a way of unloading disused pieces of equipment or making a little extra money on stuff that was just lying around anyway. But they're really invitations. They show a confidence in the passerby and in time. Someone will park on the shoulder and take a slow walk around that feed wagon, perhaps even crawl underneath it to check the running gear. Maybe not soon. But when it happens, the doorbell will ring or the dogs will bark. A stranger will present himself, someone from farther up the road, across the ridge, down the valley. The price was firm once, back when the wagon was new, a price anyone could understand. But now the wagon belongs to a different economy, which is as much a matter of tact and understanding as it is dollars and cents. It's a matter of knowing what things that have lost or long outlived their prices are really worth, stranger to stranger, neighbor to neighbor.

━━━ ≡✦≡ ━━━

The sign of full summer is a child's bicycle — the kind with a pink frame, white tires, and a white wicker basket on the handlebars — strapped to the rear end of a minivan. The van, with out-of-state plates, is parked at a pullout at Bryce Canyon National Park, in southern Utah. With his free hand a father is trying to wave his family closer to a wooden sign that marks the altitude. On the sign a raven sits, wise to the ways of tourists. The man's other hand holds a video camera.

For a few seconds the family smiles together into the lens. Behind them, beyond the hoodoos and the bristlecone pines, lies an unintelligible vastness. The family packs back into the car and drives on, to the next pullout, the next vista, the next motel or campground. The raven blinks.

This is the traveling time of year, vacation time. The campgrounds are full at all the national parks. At the major interchanges on the major transcontinental routes, the motels fill up by midafternoon. A brisk trade is being done all across the nation in plastic tomahawks and beaded coin purses, in cheeseburgers and Sno-Kones, in postcards and shrink-wrapped firewood. At the truck stops there's a sudden perplexing infusion of white-legged people who pull up to the wrong pumps and wander uninvited into the truckers' lounge. At every mountain pass a subdivision of white recreational vehicles inches its way uphill, vehicles with names like Conquest, Chieftain, and Eagle, but with satellite dishes and microwaves too.

All in all, this looks less like the quest for difference than the diffusion of sameness. Travel gets easier all the time, and it gets harder every year to distance yourself from the web of familiarity that's been thrown over the approaches to scenic America — the web of ATMs, chain restaurants, chain motels, and chain experiences. Beneath the convenience of it all lurks a hidden fear of disappointment and strangeness, of feeling displaced, of coming to the limits of a known world.

The scenery itself has been changed by so much familiarity. A vista is no longer the point of departure for an experience, the view from the trailhead, so to speak. It has become the experience. Long ago, America set out to democratize the sublime, to provide motorized access to the great natural vistas across the country. The effect has been to downsize the sublime, if only because there's no longer a sense of approach, of discovery. The trail is too well marked with souvenir shops and soft ice cream.

In a stand of trees — an acre of downed timber and blackened trunks — a three-year-old elk grazed, the velvet on his antlers still plush and unrubbed. His paunch sagged with the weight of constant feeding, and on his back sat a cowbird, heedless. The sun was still a half-hour above a knoll to the west, and in the evening light the seedheads of the grasses across the river, where the elk stood, looked ponderous, dense and purple. The river was the Gibbon, where it bends far away from the highway in a section of Yellowstone called Elk Park.

I had come to fish, and I sat with two good friends, in waders, feet dangling in the river. The fishing, highly speculative, would wait until the sun fell below the treeline and a mayfly called the brown drake appeared, if it appeared at all. Where we sat, the Gibbon flowed from west to east. Its surface, full of conflicting currents, was as bright as the fading sun. Weed beds covered the bottom, and water lilies edged the far bank. Every now and then a lily pad would turn on its side and knife downward through the water in a motion like the arc a trout makes when it rises and falls through the surface, feeding.

July

One of us would hold a hand up to the sun and watch caddis flies drifting, like the cotton from cottonwoods, across the backlit meadow, across the dark timber to the west. The elk lay down in the tall grass at the river's edge, ruminating.

After a few visits to Yellowstone you get used to the happenstance of seeing wildlife. One year the thermal meadows near the Firehole are full of bison. The next year at the same time, the flies have already driven them to higher ground. The highway through Yellowstone, to which most visitors cling, comes to seem like a lottery of sorts, a path through a set of loose probabilities — weather, season, time of day, and so on — that determine whether you'll come across a moose or a coyote or any of the other creatures whose habitations seem, to humans, entirely unfixed. To the movements of animals in Yellowstone, we naturally impute a narrow determinism — they're driven by hunger, irritation, danger, courtship. But to what do the elk in Elk Park impute our love of asphalt?

For a while, when darkness began to settle, it looked as though the brown drakes wouldn't appear. A few caddis began laying eggs on the water, slowly working their way upstream. Brown drakes are very big mayflies. They don't stroll out of the woods, like elk, or pick their way silently across a meadow, the way mouse-hunting coyotes do. They adhere to the corridor of the river as tightly as tourists adhere to pavement. They simply appear when the light is low and the air and water temperature are right.

One second the brown drakes were not there — and then there they were, fluttering up and down at head height above the Gibbon, appearing in twos and threes and then in dozens, knotting and unknotting as they mated. We were ready, waiting only for the flies to settle onto the water and cause the big brown trout living in the Gibbon to feed. The brown drakes rose and fell, rose and fell, always a little nearer to the river's surface. We looked on with a certain tension, trying at once to watch the mayflies and all of the visible river, as though it were an unmoving plane of light. Then the mayflies vanished — who knew where or why? — and the Gibbon began to flow again. We walked to the highway, where a cow elk wearing a radio collar grazed in the abrupt glow of flashbulbs.

———— ⊨◆⊨ ————

Throughout history, the moon has been a byword for mutability, its inconstancy an emblem of the inconstancy of human affairs. One night it rises dark, a new moon. One night a sliver of it hangs in the western sky, nearly catching Venus within its horns. One night it lies distended on the eastern horizon, not a sphere but a flattened disk slipping out of Earth's shadow. On no two consecutive nights has it ever risen at the same time or in the same shape. Even now, thirty years after humans first set foot on the moon, it still seems natural to attribute these qualities to the orb itself and not to the perspective we view it from.

Those who were alive then, a generation ago, will remember many things about that night, July 20, 1969. The moon was

July

a waxing crescent that just suggested the contours of its dark limb. Where skies were clear and dark, people walked outdoors and gazed at the moon, then walked back inside and looked at the scratchy black-and-white TV transmission from the landing site on the Sea of Tranquillity, then walked back outside again. Of all the imaginative leaps that occurred during the preparations for *Apollo 11,* and during the Mercury and Gemini projects, none were as difficult, because none were as abrupt, as the imaginative leap that ordinary people faced when confronted with the fact of a moon landing. And who is to say which part of that leap was harder? Realizing that two men really stood at that moment upon the moon? Recognizing the technical virtuosity and determination that had made it possible? Or understanding, for one unsettling instant, that we too, like Neil Armstrong and Buzz Aldrin, stood upon a sphere hurtling through the darkness of space?

If people groped to understand what it all meant while it was actually happening, we're still groping thirty years later. The iconic simplicity of that moment — Neil Armstrong's leap onto the moon's surface — has obscured the technical complexity, the sheer engineering will, that lay behind it. The photograph of the first American flag on the moon's surface, standing stiffly against the void of deep space, no longer suggests to us, as it did to some at the time, that America in 1969 was a nation at war with Vietnam and with itself. Looking back, I find myself wondering how it was possible to send a man from the turbulent America of the 1960s all the way to the Sea of Tranquillity.

What's most surprising about the events of that night long ago is that they're more surprising now than they were then. The breathlessness of the moment itself has subsided into mere fact. But in its place, an inescapable question has emerged. Who were we then that such a thing was possible?

◆─── ≡◆≡ ───◆

There's no such thing as a horse whisperer. There never has been and never will be. The idea is an affront to the horse. You can talk and listen to horses all you want, and what you'll learn is that they live on open ground way beyond language and that language, no matter how you characterize it, is a poor trope for what horses understand about themselves and about humans. When it comes to horses, only three things matter, patience, observation, and humility, all of which were summed up in the life of an old man who died not long ago in Northern California, a man named Bill Dorrance.

Dorrance was ninety-three, and until only a few months before his death he still rode and he still roped. He was one of a handful of men, including his brother Tom, Ray Hunt, and Buck Brannaman, who in separate ways have helped redefine relations between the horse and the human. Bill Dorrance saw that subtlety was nearly always a more effective tool than force, but he realized that subtlety was a hard tool to exercise if you believe you're superior to the horse. There was no dominance in the way Dorrance rode or in what he taught, only partnership. To the exalted horsemanship of the vaquero — the Spanish cowboy of eighteenth-century California — he brought an exalted humanity, whose highest expression is faith in the willingness of the horse.

There's no codifying what Bill Dorrance knew. Some of it, like how to braid a rawhide lariat, is relatively easy to teach, and some of it, thanks to the individuality of horses and humans, can't be taught at all, only learned. His legacy is exceedingly complex and self-annulling. It's an internal legacy. The more a horseman claims to have learned from Dorrance, the less likely he is to have learned anything at all. That sounds oblique, but it reflects the fact that what you could learn from Dorrance was a manner of learning whose subject was nominally the horse but which extended itself in surprising directions to include dogs, cattle, and people. If you really learned it, you would know it was nothing to boast about.

There's no mysticism, no magic, in this, only the recognition of kinship. Plenty of people have come across Bill Dorrance and borrowed an insight or two, and some have made a lot of money by systematizing or popularizing what they seemed to think he knew. But what he knew will never be popular, nor did he ever make much money from it. You can't sell modesty or undying curiosity. It's hard to put a price on accepting that everything you think you know about horses may change with the very next horse.

The Rural Life

⚖

This has been a rare grass year in parts of north-central Wyoming, in the drainages east of the Bighorn Mountains. As one rancher put it, "You couldn't have dialed the rains in better." The rain fell, the grass grew, the sun came out, the grass cured, and in the early weeks of July there was a kind of tonsorial fever on the hayground watered by Piney Creek, Clear Creek, and Prairie Dog Creek — men and women neatly scissoring the grass with machine-driven sickle blades. The windrows, long lines of cut grass drying in the sun, stood almost laughably high. If the profits of ranching lay in good grass instead of the vagaries of the cattle market, these ranchers would have been rich, their prosperity numbered in round bales, square bales, and enormous loaves of grass.

Everyone seemed to feel the abundance. At the Sheridan Fairgrounds a ranch roping took place one Sunday morning, a leisurely horseback competition based on the work cowboys do when branding or doctoring cattle. Once a steer was roped, head and heels, it became another rider's job to step off his horse and lay the steer down and release the ropes. But this summer the yearling steers were so fat they had no flanks to lie down upon. They lolled and bellowed and showed their great grass-fed bellies to the small crowd in the grandstand, then trotted nimbly away to rejoin the herd. Outside Sheridan, a band of riders on newly broken colts rode through an uncut field of grass, the seedheads brushing against chaps and saddles and raising the sound of the wind. Riders began to sneeze and the colts to fidget, not yet broken to the sound of sneezing.

Along every road, every path, a fringe of opulent grasses grew, ligules shading into lacquered purple, blades into the blue of dusk, awns into an almost roanlike coloration. In the waste clearings grew foxtail barley — supple, iridescent. Sagebrush rose along the fence lines in sharp-scented thunderheads. South of Sheridan, near Ucross, the hayfields are edged with sloughs, and in uncut pastures, yellow-headed blackbirds hovered momentarily before settling onto grass heads that dipped slowly beneath their weight. A buckskin horse at liberty in one of the unmowed fields showed only his back and ears, an island of contentment.

From the time the dew dried in midmorning until full dark, the windrowers moved across the fields, following the curves of the creek bottoms and the sidehills, laying the grass out in narrow rows like the isobars on a weather map. The balers followed once the grass had dried, and for a few days birds gathered on the tops of the round bales lying in the fields, looking out over a terrain that had lost much of its softness.

Then the machines came again — bale stackers for the small bales, farm trucks and tractors with hay forks for the round bales. On nearly every ranch, the hay was laid in stacks and rows where it would serve as a windbreak, a levee, in more ways than one, against winter, which suddenly seemed that much nearer once the fields were bare.

I'm writing from a screened-in porch on the north side of a house in Big Horn, Wyoming. The screens — ten panels framed in dark green — have decayed over the years. Some have ragged holes in them. Some have sagged, the result of weather and age. But each retains its power to granulate the world outside, to heighten the contrast between deep shade and the full sun on the leaves. When a finch lands on a near bough, it's like watching a Chinese painting come to life, the interwoven texture of the paper visible beneath the brush strokes. When late afternoon arrives and sunlight hits the screens, you can see only the glow of the screens themselves.

A line of saplings grows near the porch, and beyond the saplings runs a creek, and beyond the creek there's a horse pasture shaded by mature cottonwoods. The other night at twilight, as the birds were giving way to the bats, the robins set up a distracted whirring in the tallest of the cottonwoods. A great horned owl had settled on a bare bough and was calling, with a thin screech, to two more owls farther down the pasture. The screens on the porch had already deepened the night, turning the owl into a silhouette, slowly bobbing its head and shouldering its wings up around its ears.

It wasn't enough, finally, to watch from the porch. I walked out into the open air, down the pasture road, recapturing the full resolution of the darkening world, reveling in the fineness, the particularity, of sight. The owl in the tree, watching back with a gaze as keen as a dog's nose, was a soft, gray oval, barely discernible from the bark of the cottonwood in which it sat. It cried all night long, as did its fellows, and in the morning they were gone.

━━ ≡◈≡ ━━

In central Iowa the corn is head-high. It runs in perfect regimen right up to the ditches, where cattails and horsetail grass grow. No need for fences here, for there are few dissenters in a field of corn. On some farms the upright corn leaves are as dull as old paint. On others they seem to glisten, and a driver passing by at high speed in the seat of a pickup truck catches a scattered reflection skimming over the acres of seed corn like a school of fish rushing across a saltwater flat. The geometry of farming seems, if anything, a little purer in the soybean fields, where the black earth flickers between the rows. The bean fields are very clean, not a weed in sight. They are miracles of suppression as much as miracles of yield.

The gene for orderliness is visible all along the Iowa stretch of the Lincoln Highway. Near Jefferson the beans carry the trait of neatness to the edge of town, and then the headstones take over, and then the lawns and flower beds, which appear to have been mowed with barber shears and weeded with tweezers.

At the corner of Chestnut Street, a trompe l'oeil mural was painted nearly thirty years ago on the side of a building that now houses Mary Ann's Dress Shop. The mural is a view of Jefferson from out of town to the east, and it confronts a driver who has just come in from that direction with the illusion of being back where he was five minutes ago. In the painting the thunderheads are piled high, as they were one evening this week, reproducing perfectly the sensation of being squashed bug-flat by the heat.

It was so hot that night that the only thing to do was to sit in the air-conditioned pickup cab, listen to the radio, and drink root beer while the sun went bust. Across the road a few intrepid fairgoers had gathered at the Greene County fairgrounds to watch cars race on a dirt-track oval of fertile loam. The air filled with the chainsaw throttling of the cars. Songs came and went, the root beer got stale, and the air-conditioning could barely keep time with the heat, which seemed to be thickening as the darkness grew.

━━━ ⊯◈⊒ ━━

In late April a neighbor harrowed and seeded our pasture with a mixture of orchard grass, bird's-foot trefoil, clover, and rye. For weeks I looked out on a field that was uniformly brown, all its undulations exposed to view. In the silence that ensued when planting was done, I imagined a flock of starlings — a sootstorm of birds — landing on that newly planted soil and devouring every seed. That didn't happen. But as the days passed and the bare earth remained bare, I began to fear I'd neglected some vital organic precondition — a trace mineral, perhaps. Then a blush of green appeared. It was visible only if you looked across the field, and not too directly either. Faint stars at night are more easily seen if you don't stare right at them, and the same was true of the green in that field. The new shoots seemed to retire from sight if you stood right over them, questioning.

Now the pasture has been mowed once and refenced, and last night I let the horses wander through it for an hour, hock-deep in green grass. Instead of stopping to graze in any single spot, they walked briskly with their heads down, snatching a mouthful here and there as they moved. July is a month when the profusion of nature seems unbelievable, more abundant than the most verdant January daydream. The embankment bordering the gravel road is an indiscriminate, tufted mass of green. When I reset the steel T-posts around the pasture, I found a white-spun cocoon under every insulator. A caucus of earwigs had convened in the hollow behind a plastic insulator nailed to a black locust post. I took down a tent that had been standing at the edge of the woods and found that, near the summit of the tent dome, tiny ants had nested in a section of fiberglass tent pole. It was full of eggs.

In an essay called "Huckleberries," written in 1861, Henry Thoreau wrote, "Let us try to keep the new world new, and while we make a wary use of the city, preserve as far as possible the advantages of living in the country." Thoreau was talking about the need to preserve wild land not only in remote districts, but in the immediate neighborhood of our towns, to set aside "common possession" in rivers, waterfalls, lakes, hills, cliffs, and even "single ancient trees." "I do not think him fit," Thoreau said, "to be the founder . . . of a town who does not foresee the use of these things, but legislates, as it were, for oxen chiefly."

I admit that in my pasture I've been legislating for oxen. I understand Thoreau's broader point. I remain wary of the city and well aware of the advantages of living in the country. But in July, when the forest closes overhead and the air hums with the unceasing drone of insects and the pasture thickens daily underfoot, it's hard not to feel that the new world has indeed become new again. Nature does its part with an exuberance that chastens all of us.

⊷ ⊰◊⊱ ⊶

No lot is too small for delusions of grandeur. I'm thinking of Wemmick, the law clerk in Dickens's *Great Expectations*. His house in Walworth "was a little wooden cottage in the midst of plots of garden, and the top of it was cut out and painted like a battery mounted with guns." Behind the house and its drawbridge lived a pig and fowls and rabbits. There was a cucumber frame and an ornamental lake with a fountain, which "played to that powerful extent that it made the back of your hand quite wet." To Pip, the young hero of that novel,

July

Wemmick said, "I am my own engineer, and my own carpenter, and my own plumber, and my own gardener, and my own Jack of All Trades."

And when it comes to delusions of grandeur, I'm thinking of myself too, and of the nearly five acres that surround this house — ledges of rock, stands of hardwood, and open pasture. A garden is a form of managed competition, but in what remained of ours, after four years of neglect, the gloves had been removed and the ornamentals were duking it out. In a bed along the stone portico, the peonies and phlox overcame the daffodils in late spring and were now suffocating a few goosenecks and bee balms. Poppies straggled through a carpet of snow-on-the-mountain, and in front of the kitchen deck azaleas jostled against each other like cattle in a loading chute. A lilac had vaulted the roofline. The forsythia had gone insane. Where there had once been a kitchen garden, we found a few plastic plant labels — peppers mostly — littering the ground beneath a voracious thicket of mint. Everywhere the cultivars were losing to the wild species, to sumac and wild grape and wild cucumber and bindweed.

With all the clearing and pruning we had to do, not to mention waiting to see what would come up on its own, I still found myself, in April, planning a vegetable garden where I could sun myself in mid-July and say, as Wemmick did, "If you can suppose the little place besieged, it would hold out a devil of a time in point of provisions." When a demolition crew tore out the old fences, they improved the drainage in the barnyard by scraping away some topsoil, which they gathered and spread in the lee of a stone embankment, where I wanted my garden to grow. It was fertile stuff, loam of loams. I set a bench beside that quadrangle of intense, naked soil and began a beehive nearby, in the partial shade of an elderberry. The quality of my day-dreams was superb.

Now it's late July, and I can't imagine where the time went. I got busy putting up horse fence and trying not to think about the roof or the siding on the house. When I thought about the vegetable garden again, it was just a couple of days ago. I missed pea-planting time this year — early April, the soil cold but workable — and the next time I looked up I had a garden full of purple deadnettle, stinging nettles, pale smartweed, com-mon St.-John's-wort, and spotted touch-me-not, with a border of burdock and an occasional vervain thrown in. I understood for the first time that there's such a thing as defensive garden-ing, that planting corn and tomatoes and onions is also a way of forestalling the spread of unwanted species. If you don't plant, the earth will bear anyhow.

Until this summer, I'd never heard of spotted touch-me-not, which is also called jewelweed and whose botanical name is *Impatiens capensis*. It has a delicate slipper-shaped flower — orange, spotted, almost Shakespearean — which dangles from a slender stalk. *Newcomb's Wildflower Guide* calls the stem of the plant "succulent," a word which applied to roast fowl means "mouth-watering," but which used in reference to spotted touch-me-not means something like "sickeningly replete with plant juice." The name touch-me-not is ironic, when you con-sider that the sap of this plant is often used to ease the irritation of poison ivy. The name comes from the fruit, "a plump pod," says Newcomb, "that explodes when ripe." In other words, trouble. Profligate trouble too, judging from the quantity of spotted touch-me-not that grows here.

I sat on the back porch one morning with a cup of coffee, trying not to look at the decrepit porch posts. A tendril of wild cucumber spiraled upward from the branch of a peach tree. I walked down to the peach and removed the vine. I followed a path mown through the weeds to the beehive. On the way, I tugged reflectively upon a spotted touch-me-not. It came up easily. An hour and a half later, I had pulled up one of the jewelweed jungles on this place, succulence oozing from the stems, which do extract easily if you lift straight up. If you tug at an angle, they snap off at their bulbous joints with a sound like stale celery being broken. These are the kinds of things you learn when you pursue the illogic of owning an old house. You solve small problems as they come to your attention in hopes that the big problems will solve themselves.

In the ragged, harsh light of noon, the house and grounds look starkly flawed. But as the light tarries into a long July evening, I find myself counting the months and years we've been here and marveling at the changes that have taken place in that time. What still impresses me are the things that impressed me when we first came here — the sugar maples riding on a ridge of stone between two pastures, the grace of the hickories that surround the house, the soft-shoe strut of the turkeys as they come down from the woods. But the work we've done, reseeding pasture, rationalizing the fences, planting roses and apples and pears, begins to factor into my pleasure more and more. And what I notice now is that while the life around it swells with summer, rising and ebbing like a green tide, the house stands firm on its footing of stone, almost indifferent. While the herbage around it riots on midsummer nights — the wisteria fingering every weakness in foundation and porch — the house, like its owners, quietly adds another to its load of years.

August

The second cutting of hay has been postponed because the farmers can't get into the fields. If August goes on the way July has, the horses will have to eat hostas, which have never looked more prosperous. Everything fungal is having a high time of it. On yet another wet morning, with the rain disguised temporarily as fog, the bees hung in sodden mats from the hive entrances. The sky has been the color of auto primer all week long. The old metaphors for night's arrival fail. It doesn't "come," it doesn't "fall." The sun doesn't "set." The clouds merely obtrude themselves until darkness is complete. The

dogs, who are photosensitive for food, expect five o'clock supper at noon.

And so July ended. It's been like living under a rhubarb leaf.
In parts of the Northeast, the month's average rainfall fell in a
single day, disbelief rising like water in the storm drains as hour
after hour passed with no letup, the runoff gouging out driveways and washing out fields, stunting already stunted corn. The
average daily temperature for July was colder than normal by
nearly 4½ degrees in New York City, or colder by nearly 8½
degrees than last July, when we were all complaining about the
insufferable heat. It goes to show how finely attuned to normal
the human organism really is, what keen thermostats we keep
within us. At the same time, it makes normal seem like an unap-
proachable ideal, a figment of the statistician's imagination.

At a certain point, no matter how long it rains, you just have
to give up and go with it. I weed in the rain and pick blackber-
ries and blueberries in the rain. I've seen people mowing in the
rain, wearing bright yellow slickers and moving quickly to keep
the blades from jamming with wet grass. I harvested the garlic
in the garden not long ago and then found myself wondering
where I could possibly hang it to dry. Walking up the sunken
road that runs past our house, I came upon a great blue heron
airing its feet on the gravel crown. A red-tailed hawk hung
mewing in the current high overhead, just to feel the breeze.

Above the hawk and above the cloud cover the sun is shining brightly, tipping now toward evening and Scorpio's rise. I
think of a kind of photomachy going on up there, a struggle
between light and dark, the sun trying to pierce the clouds,

August

while the clouds, infinitely mutable, block the sun's energies. It's something Rubens would paint, a masterpiece of effulgence and protuberance, a Baroque battle scene in whose shadow the ordinary lives of ordinary people go steadily on, while they wait to see how it will all turn out.

———— ≋✦≋ ————

Wyoming is a metropolis of clouds. Some are born in the state, some move here from other places, but they all prosper, because Wyoming is also a theater of wind. For days at a time this summer, the clouds have passed in migratory flight, complicating the sunlight. In late afternoon especially, along the northeastern rim of the Bighorn Mountains, great rafts of orographic clouds — shaped by the mountains, that is — rise with the terrain and then lean out over the creek bottoms, darkening the face of the Bighorns and reabsorbing that darkness.

It's been a wet summer in Wyoming, and rich in cloud life. Hay bales have been stacked in pyramids in the fields to keep the damp off, and the barley has gone unirrigated. Often enough, when morning dawns, the dogs run up the hayfield road, inhaling and exhaling cloud, until they vanish into even grayness.

Those are the usual summer days, which often turn cloudless by noon. They end with lightning flickering all around the night horizon, the storms so distant that they lie beneath the constellation Scorpio, which never gets very high in the sky this far north. But along the road from Cheyenne to Sheridan a squall line blew in from the open prairie to the east, an ominous, upward-thrusting shield of precipitation. The temperature dropped nearly thirty degrees, and the rain fell against the direction of the wind so heavily that drivers pulled off the road, turned off their wipers, and watched the lightning take dead aim around them.

Twenty miles down the road, the temperature rose as much as it had fallen. The squall line broke apart into a landscape of sky that beggared the landscape of earth. Clouds congealed into innumerable shapes, each requiring its own analogy. Shards of flint and flakes of obsidian knifed through the middle atmosphere. Mammatus clouds, as smoothly pebbled as a low-water beach, clung to the underside of thunderheads, while pileus clouds — the name means skullcap — clung to their tops.

Some clouds had become castellated, and others had been beaten into sheets of lead or folded back upon themselves again and again like Damascus steel. The galactic gas jets of the deep universe were present and so were the nebulae. So too was the tight, blue-tinted hairdo of a matron marching westward in dudgeon across the sky. She canted over the sagebrush flats, hit an updraft, and was teased into nothingness.

August

I've been stung by nettles so often this summer that my hands have reached a state of continuous numbness — not so numb, however, that I can't feel the next nettle bite. I go down without gloves to the vegetable garden in early morning when the dew is still thick, planning only to drink my coffee and watch the potatoes grow. But new nettles have always sprung up overnight, and old ones that lay hidden in the hops reveal themselves in the low sun. I can't help plucking them, even barehanded. *Weeds of the Northeast*, that indispensable book, prints a lurid photo of a nettle's stinging hairs. It adds, "When the tip of the hair is broken off on contact with the skin, it acts as a hypodermic needle, injecting the toxins histamine, acetylcholine, and 5-hydroxytryptamine into the wound." Nettles prefer rich soil, so I acknowledge the compliment and heave them onto the compost pile.

On a terrace above the potatoes, a pumpkin plant has wound its way into the sweet corn. So have the vines of the cherry tomatoes, some winter squash, and three cucumber plants — two cukes too many. I step into this maze of vines and stalks every day just to enjoy its architecture and to admire the clutching and grasping going on in the narrow dirt streets beneath the cornstalks. This part of the garden isn't the least bit pastoral. All the vining plants have their hackles up. Their leaves and stems bristle and rasp against the skin as I shift them about, while trying not to step on the cucumbers, which are armored with stiff spurs. The common mellifluousness of spring's new growth is long gone. Everyone in the garden is a character now, for better or worse.

Ripeness is just a form of specialization, or a specialization of form. Either way, it's descending upon this garden quickly now, like dusk creeping a little nearer every day. It seems like an incredible extravagance to wait so long, so patiently, for an ear of sweet corn or a ripe tomato. The wait is nearly over. I almost expect a pause when ripeness comes, but the garden will rush forward into senescence, or rather into its own definition of ripeness instead of mine. A broccoli has already bolted. The pea vines are stiff and brown. The pole beans have begun to wilt. Japanese beetles have eaten nearly all of the Virginia creeper that steals from the upper garden into the lower one. Only the nettles continue to come up spring green every day, the nettles, the lamb's-quarters, and the jewelweed.

⋅━ ⛏ ━⋅

This is a good hopper year in the West, if you happen to like hoppers, a year of subscourge abundance. In an unscientific study conducted late last afternoon, I discovered that if you walk with two dogs across a level, sixty-acre Wyoming pasture, you kick up a gross of hoppers with every step, never mind what the dogs dislodge. One of the dogs, a yellow mutt, lunges at the hoppers that leap into her path, mouths them, and spits them out, blinking. The other dog is too stately for hoppers. When horses walk through the tall, dry grass, they lower their heads and weave them back and forth, watching the insects fan out beneath their feet, listening to the sudden eruption, which sounds like high wind among brittle leaves or the very distant call of a kingfisher.

The birds love the sudden proliferation. You usually see robins tugging at earthworms as though they were anchor chains, but now the robins run along the edges of gravel roads, picking off hoppers as they go. There's a lot of extra protein available, which is good for the grouse and pheasants and good for the trout patrolling the stream banks. In the morning, as the sun is getting strong, the hoppers climb from the high grass onto the eastern walls of ranch buildings, where they wait until they're fully charged, ready to go off. They're easy to capture in the morning.

A grasshopper will cling to the end of your finger, trying always to keep itself out of the line of sight. Seen in profile, there's a muted, almost Italianate beauty to a grasshopper. It looks embossed, machined, any one of its body parts raised only slightly above the others. A rich herringbone pattern runs along the enormous thigh, and the stubby, segmented antennae darken outward from the head to a deep sienna. Look near enough and it's possible to see your own reflection in the impassive, oval eye.

I wonder what the ants make of it all. Somehow, out here in the West, the grasshopper seems more sympathetic than he does in the old fable. The difference between an ant and a grasshopper is that a grasshopper believes in posterity while an ant prefers immediate family. What's so improvident about grazing all summer, waiting for wings, and then laying dozens of eggs that will hatch when winter has come and gone and you've come and gone with it? Somehow, out here, it seems preferable to expire alone on the high prairie, as a grasshopper will, than to die, as the ants do, in a hole among many thousands of your kind.

A few days ago, at the edge of a desolate mall in New York's Mohawk Valley, I saw a young Amish woman sitting on the back end of a horseless carriage — horseless because the horse was elsewhere. She was selling sweet corn. Everyone is selling sweet corn right now and selling it with an almost touching earnestness, knowing that this is the season of sweet corn glut. I've come across a few ears and a coffee can for a cash till lying on a board beside a garden. I've seen children's wagons mounded with dark ears parked on the sidewalk. At some of the bigger roadside stands, it looks as if the proprietors were really selling brown paper bags and using the corn to hold them up. The bags absorb the moisture the corn gives off and collapse while being carried into the house. Everyone says the best way to prepare sweet corn is to remove it from the stalk, husk it on the way to the kitchen, and drop it into already boiling water. I get good results if I drive it home, drop it on the lawn when the bag breaks, and then prepare as usual.

In a place like the Mohawk Valley, where some large-scale farming is still being done, sweet corn is nearly always being sold within sight of fields full of field corn, the kind marked near the fence line by a seed company sign and a number. The number registers the type of seed planted there, which may be, among other possibilities, a white, yellow, high-oil, extractable-starch, or silage corn. The number also marks a way out of the trap that sweet corn inventors are in, who are obliged to think up names like Bodacious, Calico Belle, Maverick, and Zenith.

The roadside sweet corn grows in patches, gardens, and, sometimes, a good-sized stand of plowed ground. The dent corn, the stuff in the fields, grows in landscapes. It's as much architecture as agriculture, an architecture that has grown more and more grandiose. In an Amish field, I saw a horse-drawn one-row corn picker. Here and there, abandoned along fence lines, you sometimes see rusted four- and eight-row pickers — the kind that fit over the cowl of a tractor like some kind of medieval horse armor. Out in the irrigated corn forests of central Nebraska, there are corn-picking heads for combines that are far too wide for the highways.

Forty years ago, the field corn seemed widely spaced and somehow personable enough to hide in, the way Cary Grant did in *North by Northwest*. You couldn't edge your way into some modern fields. The corn they're seeded with comes in pallets full of bags holding 80,000 kernels each and plants out at around 30,000 kernels per acre. In the dense river-bottom fields along the Mohawk River, all that corn is nearing a biological climax. It won't be picked for another two months, but it's now coming into the last of the green, those final weeks before the leaves and stalks begin the slow browning of autumn. Every field looks like an army of aspirants, leaves flung skyward in a kind of hosanna.

I was stung by a honeybee on the back of the head while weeding in the garden one afternoon. There was nothing surprising about being stung, since upward of 100,000 bees live about thirty feet from where I was working. I could hear the droning of the hives and smell the sweet, waxy scent that emanates from a healthy colony. The air high above my head was thick with bee traffic homing downward out of the east at a velocity that's not easily credible unless you've actually seen it. Still, I resented being stung. "After all I've done for you," was my first thought, a sign that I haven't quite matured as a beekeeper. But it wasn't even the sting that I resented. It was the slap of an angry bee — a suicidal bee — against my scalp and the knowledge that she had decided at a distance to poison me.

I was stooped over in the weeder's posture, left forearm resting on my left knee, right hand wrapped around a rosette of burdock leaves, my head exposed only in that small half-moon between the back of the baseball cap I was wearing and its adjustable strap. I had decided the burdock was a weed, and the bee had decided I was a threat. The bee sting flared up with that familiar white heat and then faded abruptly away. Unless you're allergic, it's much more satisfying to be stung by a bee than by a mosquito. There's none of that cautious, reluctant, hovering parasitism — that sneaking effort to steal some blood and then fly away. What a bee is really good at is transmitting hostility.

I must have looked like a bear to that bee. The beekeepers I know have trouble with bears, which take an almost orgiastic pleasure in scattering a hive's contents. When a bear visits an apiary, it looks as though the bear planted a bomb and then retreated to the edge of the woods to detonate it. Perhaps bears like the salt of the stings as much as they love the sweet of the honey and the taste of the wax and the white brood lying in their cells. We haven't seen any bears around here — yet — largely because of a busy road and horses and dogs and an electric fence. That doesn't keep the bees from being bear-wary in their ancestral way.

But late one night not long ago — one of the most beautiful nights this summer — a black bear crossed the road just in front of us as we were driving home through southern Vermont. It was the fragile end of dusk. Out of thick, sloping cover on the far side of the road, the bear burst at a lope, visible for only as long as it took to clear the road. But that was long enough to see that its fur was the same color as the night sky and that the gloss on its fur had the same effect as stars shining out in the night. We coasted through its vapor trail, and if we could have, we would have smelled its very bearness. It was the only thing to think about all the rest of the way home.

＊＋ ⟫◈⟪ ＋＊

For the past few years I've driven west every summer, and every summer the question returns: Where does the West begin? There are plenty of commonsense answers, the kind that break this country up into regions as neatly defined as the pieces in a child's wooden puzzle. If it were just a matter of political boundaries, I wouldn't look for the West before the Colorado border. And if it were just a matter of mood, the West would begin in upstate New York on the day I walk the horses into the horse trailer, check the running lights one more time, and pull away into the fog of dawn.

The mind travels so much faster than a pickup truck hauling two humans, two dogs, two horses, and all their gear in a gooseneck trailer. The first day we come to the farms and factories southwest of Toledo. Rural roads dwindle to a single paved lane, and cars, meeting each other, drive half on a gravel track and half on the asphalt. A dank, sulfurous glow hangs over the truck stops and drive-ins near the Maumee River and the town of Napoleon, Ohio. The question of where the West begins is mooted, for the moment. It's just another way of asking, When will we get there?

But by early afternoon the next day — western Illinois, eastern Iowa — I get momentary glimpses of a setting that carries me westward a thousand miles at once. It's usually a pasture threaded by a creek, rare enough in an empire of soybeans and corn. Cattle wander among the trees, one or two of the trunks rubbed bare, bone white. The scene flashes across my eyes, raising the picture of a similar place along Wyoming's Tongue River or Crazy Woman Creek. Then the corridor of corn resumes, row after row flickering past in the wet August light.

When the polite undulations of Iowa are past and we start the slow westward uptilt of Nebraska, the search for the West begins in earnest. Is it a copse of cottonwoods in a creek bottom? The first herd of horses where roans and duns predominate? I'm always surprised, driving across Nebraska, that no one thought to mark the hundredth meridian, somewhere between Cozad and Gothenburg, a well-known line of demarcation between the humid East and the semiarid West. But in Nebraska they irrigate the cornfields, and so the difference, in vegetation at least, is diminished.

Beyond North Platte, nearing Ogallala, the West begins to win out over the Midwest. The mileage signs give distances to Cheyenne and Denver instead of Chicago and Des Moines. The low hills in the distance begin to be ridged with pines and the farms start to look like ranches. Yet something is still missing, some defining marker. Sagebrush would do, or a small wilderness of yucca or prickly pear. And there, in the fields ahead, is the answer. Now I remember, for the answer is the same every year, on this highway at least. The West begins where they put hay up in stacks.

September

Beside a county road near the town of Hygiene, Colorado, stands a cottonwood that turned completely yellow the second week of August. To southbound cyclists that tree lies hidden, lurking beneath a sharp dip in the road. They coast along in summer's full incumbency — the scent of hay practically creasing their foreheads — when all at once the asphalt slopes away, and that lone cottonwood presents itself, its leaves shimmering in a bright wind that suddenly seems autumnal, full of the brittleness, the clarity, of fall.

It's not as though anyone goes searching for autumn in the midst of summer. In most of America those seasons have reversed their traditional, agricultural meanings. Summer is now the harvest season — a harvest of leisure, of fresh vegetables from the garden. The onset of autumn has become an occasion for brisk renewal, and Labor Day, not the autumnal equinox, is the hinge on which those seasons now swing. I try to ignore the signs of summer's end — the drying milkweed in the fields, the reddening sumac along the railroad tracks, the schoolbuses. But sooner or later there's a sign too portentous to ignore.

A few nights ago an enormous flight of blackbirds emerged from the shadow of the Bighorn Mountains. The blackbirds flew across open pasture and out over the low ground where Little Goose Creek flows. From the bluff overlooking the creek, I could see for a moment what shape the flock had taken. It was a lens of blackbirds. It neared the crown of a great cottonwood, and suddenly one bird, then another, plunged downward, dying on the wing it seemed, into the branches. The flock swirled, then settled. There was a momentary hush. Then, as if a school bell had sounded, the tree erupted in chatter, which rang out across the high ground.

After a sight like that I'm almost ready for autumn. But not quite. The days are still hot in Wyoming, the evenings warm, the skies full of dry thunder. The ranchers are beginning to move cattle to the sale yards and railheads — a sure sign of fall — but summer will reign for at least a few more days. I drive east of Sheridan, just to catch the evening, and wind up chasing a Burlington Northern coal train at sunset past the grade crossings at Dutch Center and East Dutch, past the old grain elevator at Wyarno. There the pavement ends, and the train pulls ahead, its new aluminum coal cars gleaming in the last of the light. I stop on a rise to watch the train slip away into the next valley, out among the round bales stacked in windbreaks. As the rumble of the train disappears, the crickets persist, and in their voices it's high summer all over again.

—⊷ ⋝◆⋝ ⊷—

In 1875 a photographer named Alphonse Deriaz took a picture of the Butchers' Festival in the town of Morges, Switzerland. The butchers, twenty-six of them, stand at attention in the town square, their aprons swept to one side like dashing military tunics. Each man shoulders one of the tools of his trade. Five of the butchers share a raised platform with an enormous white-faced bullock wearing a halter and a crown of flowers while townsfolk look down from the windows above. What's striking here, besides the soft expression on the bullock's face, is the very public way that each butcher identifies himself by his labor, by his apron and bone-saw, and by the fraternity, publicly attested, of fellow butchers.

The festival this photograph preserves feels Old World, utterly unlike a modern American Labor Day, which is now less a celebration of labor than one last gasping infusion of summer's ozone. But police officers and firefighters and union members and politicians still march together through the city

The Rural Life

streets on this day. It would be something to see the butchers of
New York marching too, dressed for work — to see them and
the sommeliers and the toll takers and the men and women
who build wooden water tanks and each of the vocations that
gives flesh to this society marching side by side, a society articu-
lated, for one parade, into all its laboring parts.

What's Old World about the Butchers' Festival isn't only the
uniforms and the ability to look the source of meat right in the
eye. It's the sense of lifelong calling, of a time when going to
work meant assuming, for life, an identity as binding, if perhaps
not as deranging, as Bartleby the scrivener's. The days when
men and women bore the distinguishing marks of their labor
have certainly not ended, nor will they ever end as long as the
material world is shaped in part by human muscle. But now we
seem as migratory in our vocations as we do in our dwelling
places, as ready to shift jobs as to shift cities. There's a familiar,
prevailing sense that no matter what the job, it's probably too
small to contain something as volatile and transcendent as our
latter-day identities — made up, we seem to believe, of finer
stuff than those of our ancestors.

Labor is both trap and liberation, servitude and release, and
it's tempting to think of labor — even the word itself — in
largely historical terms, to remember photographs from a century ago of coal-darkened miners and young women huddled
over sewing machines, of factory workers looking up from the
conveyor belt at the photographer's flash. But there's nothing
historical about these labors. They're still being performed
today. Where the world of work is concerned, we still dwell

142

among our ancestors. Some people dream of living in a world without work. But the better dream, even on a day as relaxed as Labor Day, is that of a world in which everyone has the work he wants.

— ‹›== ‹ —

Not long after the sun burns out, some 5 billion years from now, the galaxy we live in may collide with the Andromeda Galaxy (M31). For now the Andromeda Galaxy remains pretty much where it's always been found in human experience: 2.2 million light years away and a few degrees below and to the right of the conspicuous, W-shaped constellation called Cassiopeia, which lies halfway up the northeastern sky about bedtime this season of the year. The impending collision of these two galaxies — the catastrophic intersifting of six or seven hundred billion stars and all their attendant worlds — is the kind of celestial happening that belongs on everyone's worry list. A person would do well to resolve to fret about nothing less significant or less distant than an event of this magnitude. Compared to that, the sun's flaming out is a bagatelle.

At least that's how it seems when I lie in a Wyoming hay field looking up at the sky on a warm September night. In the near distance, the lights of Sheridan cast a benign glow, and in the far distance — as far, in fact, as the unaided eye can see — M31 dispels its faint cloud of light. It's the kind of night in which the constellations seem like old friends. Scorpio — the Scorpion — has hooked its tail into the Bighorn Mountains. Delphinus — the Dolphin — surfs in the foamy crest of the Milky Way. Sagittarius — the Bowhunter in this part of the world — lies at the place where the Milky Way plunges into the Bighorns, and it marks, as well, the center of our galaxy, whose brightness is obscured by clouds of dust.

In the cottonwood draw where Little Goose Creek flows, deer cough from time to time and a great horned owl screeches punctually. A cricket in the hay stubble emits a pure, intermittent, staccato whine that could as well be the sound of some pulsar deep in the recesses of the universe. The horses that live in this field keep their distance, but I can feel their presence, a weight and a wariness nearly as palpable as the breeze that stirs the grasses. It's almost time for Saturn to rise, a bright spot (scarcely eight hundred million miles away) climbing into the sky just below M31, whose light tonight is as ancient as the oldest stone tools ever found on Earth. On a night this clear, near and far, past and future, seem almost to merge, bisected only by the observer.

I blew a tire on the pickup not long ago between Lander and Riverton, Wyoming. The truck and horse trailer coasted to a stop on a slight rise, on a stretch of highway within sight of a cluster of pastel houses on the Wind River Reservation. In the distance, in a different direction, lay Riverton itself, a town, coincidentally, with more tire stores for its size than any other place I've ever been. To the west lay the mountains of the Wind River Range. While I put on the spare, I began wondering whether the indistinct rise I was parked on had ever been given a name. If I had hiked a tenth of a mile up the road, I would have come upon a highway marker giving my exact numerical location on that stretch of asphalt. But that's not the same as a name.

To drive around the West, as I've been doing for the past few weeks — visiting friends and ranchers — is to drop again and again from an approximate geography into a highly specific one. I set my route by the red or black lines, sometimes even the faint gray ones, in the road atlas. But when the day is over and the horses are unloaded, Lindy and I find ourselves in the company of a rancher who tells his son how to locate a stray cow by saying, "across Butcher Creek where we saw the bear this spring." Place becomes a question of time and incident, not maps, no matter how fine their scale.

In a way, that local sense of place can't be mapped. It depends too much on experience. I understood this when I saw the Chief Joseph Trail in the Clark's Fork Canyon of Wyoming — a delicate thread of a trail as steep and narrow as a crow's-foot at the corner of a weathered eye. The Nez Percé fled along that path, which climbs high above the canyon and vanishes again and again. At a place called Big Sand Coulee, I met a woman who drives her cattle along that trail each June to her forest grazing permit. She rides her horse where it's hard to imagine making your way on foot.

In Lander, my nephew Jake, a first grader, brought me to show-and-tell. He introduced me to the other students in Mrs. Foxley's class at South School, and I showed them on a map of the United States just how far I had driven to be there. It was an old-fashioned schoolroom map that unfurled like a window blind and contained a striking absence of detail. I placed my finger where Lander would be, below the y in Wyoming. One boy asked, "Where's Fort Washakie?" All I could do was point to the very same spot. It seemed, at the moment, like an absurd answer, for every student in that classroom knew that Fort Washakie lies only a few miles north, where the highway crosses the Little Wind River and begins to climb toward Dubois.

A hot southerly wind blew through central Wyoming recently, disturbing the dogs and turning the cottonwood leaves silver side out. A small forest fire had been burning for days near Stockwell Creek in the Bighorn Mountains. It had nearly been extinguished when the wind blew the fire over Little Goose Peak and onto the steep walls of an adjacent canyon. What had been a narrow plume a few hours earlier was now an inverted pyramid of smoke, its source steadily broadening, its edges keenly incised by the wind in an otherwise perfectly blue sky.

September

The smoke streamed northward over the town of Big Horn, a few miles away, which had grown distracted. A woman who had just come off the fire line walked up and down the stairs beside the Mercantile, Big Horn's general store, unable to remember what she had wanted there in the first place. The doors of the fire station stood open, and there was a puzzling air of expectant idleness about the place, which was resolved the next morning when exhausted fire crews, eating white bread and bologna sandwiches, gathered in clumps outside the station. The whole town seemed to be living under the fumarole of an active volcano.

It was impossible that afternoon to do much else but watch the smoke. Along the east-west face of the Bighorns, the wind sucked the lower edge of the smoke cloud downward, out over the hay meadows and pastures south of town. It looked as though the sky were full of deep-dyed virgas, falsely promising a smoky rain. The central mass of the smoke pillar was tinted a livid yellow — the color of wheat fields at twilight — and when I stood in its shadow I seemed to be standing in the eerie light of a partial eclipse. Even when I wandered into full sunlight, the atmosphere possessed a new chromatic intensity.

By night from the precincts of Big Horn, I could see only a dull red glow, like the moon rising behind a thin layer of clouds. Then the wind would shift, and the flames, burning in six or seven spots across the north face of the canyon, would come unveiled for a minute or two. Trucks and cars were returning from the mountains along the road called Red Grade, and compared to the headlights — so piercing, so focused — the fire seemed to burn with a blunt incandescence. But soon smoke settled over the canyon again, and the heat of the fire, its roar, and now even its light were lost in the distance. What remained in the darkness was a hot wind and the smell of ashes.

Around Sheridan, Wyoming, everyone has been talking about winter all summer. At the Big R, a ranch supply store on the edge of town, the aisles are filled with forecasts. "They say it's going to be harder than last winter," the ranchers and store clerks declare, and if the weight of rumor is any measure of truth, there's a dire season coming.

But no one really knows. Judging the harshness of winter before Labor Day is like trying to predict cattle prices two years down the road. Some will guess right and some will guess wrong, and the fever of speculation won't for an instant be quelled. In ranch country it's never too soon to wonder about the next season of snow and ice. Cows have long since been pregnant with the calves that will come before winter has blown away.

In Wyoming people talk as though winter were "out there" even now, lurking not in time but in space, being prepared somewhere in a shop or factory, awaiting only final assembly and shipment to the proper address. Talk like that is a gesture of submission, and a reflection somehow of the topographical openness of the state. Also, that talk is a way for people to remind one another of what they've already gone through together and are prepared to go through again — just part of the cost of being neighbors in a landscape so spare of humans but so full of weather.

Still, what's striking about all these rumors of a hard winter to come is their capacity to transform the scenery now. It's been a cool, wet summer around Sheridan, and the hills carry the green of late June, not the brown of the end of September. The cottonwoods have only lately started to catch the rattle of autumn. But I can't help standing in the hay fields and imagining the red snout of winter, the white shock of its hair, beginning to poke over the Bighorn Mountains.

"Not much of a summer," people have been saying for weeks at the Mercantile in Big Horn. They mean that there have been very few days when a person could pretend that July would last forever. This summer was mortal from the start.

----- ≖♦≖ -----

The days shorten, the morning chill intensifies, and all across the Rockies cattle have been driven down from the high country. Ranchers on horseback gathered before dawn at the mouth of a canyon along Clark's Fork of the Yellowstone River to drive 193 yearling steers and one Corriente bull down the highway to a set of corrals — a trip of thirteen miles — where they would be weighed, given a clean bill of health, and trucked to feedlots in Kansas. The night before, some of the cattle had moved down the highway on their own, only to follow the wind back up into the canyon in early morning. The herd was footsore.

At sunrise the steers were on the move. The highway dropped eastward out of the mountains, where the wind was hard, and into a still basin that quickly filled with morning sun. From time to time I turned to hasten a laggard steer and caught a glimpse of dawn reflected against the mountain walls. Several men rode ahead of the herd, and as they came upon openings in the highway fence they positioned their horses abreast of them to keep the steers from breaking through into the open country beyond.

Wherever the sage and chamisa gave way to grass, the cattle would bunch up eating, and wherever their path crossed irrigation ditches, they would wallow and bawl, and then the blacktop would be traced with long sinuous lines of drool. But mostly the yearlings were quiet, almost stoic. From a distance their feet moving through stiff grass sounded like spring rain. In their silence they were completely unlike a herd of cow-calf pairs.

The night before, one of the horsemen had moved a herd of mother cows and their calves from one pasture into the next, a trip of perhaps five hundred yards. The word "moo" doesn't do justice to the cries that filled the evening air. As the cries rose and fell and rose again, they began to sound like the tintinnabulation of bells on a feast day in some medieval city. Then the last calf was driven through the gate, its mother found, and the night was no louder than the wind across the hilltops.

September

The tomato cages have been toppled by the latest storm — yet more rain in a rainy summer. Japanese beetles have pinholed the raspberries and the rhubarb and the leaves of a Montmorency cherry. The roses and hollyhocks are in tatters too. It's late summer, and I can almost feel the organic inertia overwhelming the vegetable garden — the outsized cucumbers, the bolted lettuce, the ever-bearing strawberries making their break from the raised beds. I planted the dark side of the garden in squash and pumpkins, and for a few weeks the seedlings grew hardly at all. Then in early July someone fired a starter's gun, and the race was on. The French pumpkins have overtaken the butternut squash, and they are all bearing down in a dead heat on the hops arbor, where the hops have lapped the climbing roses. So much growth looks surprisingly like decay. The end is in sight.

A gardener anticipates the mortality of his vegetable garden. By early fall, it's somehow the point. My own garden nearly always ends in fresh wilderness. In autumn I stare at the demise of my spring plans and realize that the great sadness and great joy of vegetable gardening is that so few vegetables are perennial where I live. All those drawings and plottings come down to this, a cornucopia of nettles and soon-to-be-frostbit tomatoes. The fullest ambition of the northern kitchen gardener is to see the wrack of his old garden moldering in a compost heap, ripening for next spring.

Other gardens — the kinds with conifers and obelisks and classical fountains, with avenues of pleached trees and files of boxwood — are planted in homage to continuity. But even those gardens, those enduring works of imagination and design and ambition, don't last forever. Not long ago I came across a passage in Goethe's journal of his voyage to Italy that says something substantial about the way even lofty gardens come to an end. The date is September 21, 1786, and Goethe is in Vicenza, still in his first intoxication with Italy. He writes:

Today I visited Doctor Turra; for some five years he concentrated passionately on botany, assembled a herbarium of Italian flora, and, under the previous bishop, established a botanical garden. But that is all past. Natural history was replaced by medical practice, the herbarium is food for worms, the bishop is dead, and the botanical garden has been replanted, as is proper, with cabbages and garlic.

The bishop dies, and that's that. Under the next bishop, food for the scientist's mind becomes food for the cleric's stomach, "as is proper." Goethe gives every garden its epitaph: "But that is all past."

So gardens end with the bishop's death and with the worms. They end in a hard frost and in a drought. They end where the neighbor's property begins or at the limit of the drip-irrigation line or where the woods close in. They end in a view, a wall, a border, a road, a tangle of weeds, a subdivision, or in political turmoil, a change of ownership, a reversal of fortune. They end where energy and money and ideas run out, or where the deer and woodchucks begin. They end in divorce and death. They end most happily by beginning all over again.

And sometimes gardens end abruptly, violently, in a cataclysm, natural or otherwise. A few months ago I was reading John Ruskin's strange, late work called *Fors Clavigera,* a series of long, fulminating letters addressed to "the Workmen and Labourers of Great Britain," whom he hoped to form into a utopian society called the Guild of St. George. In the fifth letter of *Fors Clavigera,* dated December 1871, Ruskin writes about Goethe's theory that a plant's parts are merely variations of each other — that, in Ruskin's words, "all the parts of a plant had a kind of common nature, and would change into each other." Goethe put it more succinctly. "Everything is leaf," he wrote.

For Ruskin the idea that "there are no such thing as Flowers — there are only gladdened Leaves" is an attractive one, but he believed that in the hands of scientists the idea became a misperception, a misreading of the plant's purpose, which is to produce flowers. His mistrust of science is unequivocal. "You have learned," he wrote,

> that there is no such thing as a flower; and as far as your scientific hands and scientific brains, inventive of explosive and deathful, instead of blossoming and life-giving, Dust, can contrive, you have turned the Mother-Earth, Demeter, into the Avenger-Earth, Tisiphone — with the

voice of your brother's blood crying out of it, in one wild harmony round all its murderous sphere.

As a footnote, Ruskin quotes a letter to the *Times* of London, dated April 5, 1871, from the great English garden designer William Robinson. Robinson had gone to Paris to see what the Franco-Prussian War had done to the gardens there. In September 1870 the German army laid siege to Paris, and during the winter the city consumed itself. Some forty thousand oxen and a quarter-million sheep grazed in the Bois de Boulogne, but they were not enough. The city grew cold and dark and hungry that winter. A French Horticultural Relief Fund had been raised to repair war damage to French gardens, but it was clear to Robinson that the money would fall far short of the need. Most of Paris's public gardens had survived the siege, Robinson reported, but along the Avenue de l'Impératrice "a sad scene of desolation presents itself." What was once "the finest avenue garden in existence" was now, he stated dryly, "as cheerless as Leicester Square or a sparsely furnished rubbish yard." It was hardly surprising. "After a similar ordeal," he wrote, "we should not have a stick left in London."

Grand Parisian gardens, though, weren't the only ones to be decimated in the winter of 1870–71. "When at Vitry on the 28th of March," Robinson noted, "I found the once fine nursery of M. Honoré Dufresne deserted, and many acres once covered with large stock and specimens cleared to the ground." Near one village Robinson came upon an embankment built to protect an artillery battery. It was made up of "mattresses, sofas, and almost every other large article of furniture, with the earth stowed between. There were, in addition, nearly forty orange and oleander tubs gathered from the little gardens in the neighbourhood visible in various parts of this ugly bank." Robinson wrote: "Multiply these few instances by the number of districts occupied by the belligerents during the war, and some idea of the effects of glory on gardening in France may be obtained."

Thoughts of war, even distant, long-forgotten wars, are the kind of thoughts that gardeners try instinctively to exclude from their meditations. So many natural forces prey upon a garden over time that it's hardly worth thinking about the unnatural forces that might also do so, the ones that by Robinson's estimate destroyed some two and a half million young trees around two villages near Paris in a single winter. But I find myself thinking again and again about the way Robinson links glory and gardening. "Glory" is his shorthand for military esprit, the zeal for conquest and blood sacrifice. It makes an interesting juxtaposition, glory and gardening, if not a perfect antithesis.

I wonder, for instance, what it must have been like for a veteran of World War I, supremely a war of excavation, to have turned his first peacetime spadeful of soil in some quiet cottage garden during the spring of 1919, the first spring after the armistice. What must the bite of the spade have felt like to him? How immaculate, almost virginal, must the earth in those few square meters of home garden have seemed after the squalid soil along the front lines in France and Belgium, where large parts of former battlegrounds are still cordoned off, where bits of bone and metal, explosives and debris, are still being disinterred nearly a century later. That indeed is Ruskin's Avenger-Earth, the evil garden.

In December 1999 severe storms swept northern Europe and blew down some ten thousand trees at Versailles, many of them nearly two hundred years old. The news photographs of the destruction at Versailles looked like the early stages of a bombardment, the woods toppled, the earth not yet plowed into mud by the shells. But those photographs also resembled a pair of eighteenth-century paintings by the artist and garden designer Hubert Robert. When Louis XVI came to the throne in 1774, the various woods at Versailles, the bosquets, were in terrible repair. They had been planted with mature trees ripped from forests in Compiègne and Normandy at the end of the seventeenth century. It fell to the new king to undo his predecessors' neglect, and he ordered the removal of several of the old bosquets and the planting of new groves in a less formal, English style.

Robert, whose patron was also one of the king's horticultural counselors, was commissioned to paint two different scenes of the destruction, both of which were exhibited in 1777. One is called *View of Apollo's Wood During the Felling of the Trees*. Robert was famous for his love of architectural ruins, but in this painting the ruins are botanical. Apollo's Wood is a scene of industry and chaos. A work crew tugs at a rope attached well up the trunk of a tree being felled. A sawyer works his way along the length of a downed tree. Men of military demeanor survey the scene, as do ladies of fashion.

The more interesting painting of that event is Robert's view of the felling of trees near the Tapis Vert, with a glimpse of the Grand Canal receding into the distance. Children play on an impromptu seesaw. Woodsmen and their axes rest against the base of a statue and the carcass of a tree. The king and queen stand in the right foreground, looking over the arboreal upheaval. Somehow there's a tension in this painting that's missing in its companion piece. Partly it's the grotesquerie of the trees themselves — enormous hulks of wood — towering over the colonnade in the distance, over great urns, over a statue of Milo of Crotona being devoured by a lion, his hand caught in the trunk of a tree. It's a scene right out of William Gaddis's *JR*, where trees "appeared to stagger without even provocation of a breeze, rearing their splintered amputations in all directions."

But the real tension in this painting comes from the presence of Louis XVI and Marie Antoinette. They transform this scene of destruction and revelry into a moment of overlap between two worlds, that of the woodsmen, axes at rest, and that of the king and his consort, who would feel the blade on their necks some seventeen years later. The interest of the painting is its faint horror, the sense of botanical carnage and social inversion, even though what Robert witnesses is a new approach to order, a reinvestment in the park, and workmen resting under the eyes of their employer and king. It's a view of peaceable destruction, but in the very restoration of those bosquets there is also a glimpse of the end of the lineage that planted them, though Robert could not have known it.

That moment in Versailles — the felling of those trees — was merely a minor adjustment in a garden that even then belonged to history, a garden already more than a century old. Robert's painting is both a documentary and a Shakespearean fantasy, a comedy in which the court ventures into a wood where disorder prevails, where ruin is imminent but always forestalled, where decay suggests not the past but the future. Catherine the Great, who tried unsuccessfully to bring Robert to Russia, remarked that he preferred to live in what she called a land of ruins, which is what revolutionary France would become. Denis Diderot, the art critic and Encyclopedist, tried to explain the psychological effect of Robert's fascination with ruins. It was, he said, a fascination with endings and the transformation they bring. "How old the world is!" Diderot imagined Robert thinking. "I walk between two eternities."

Yet the world isn't old for everyone, and on the American plains the two eternities aren't past and future, but grass and sky. I have my own personal pendant to Robert's painting. It's a print of a work called *Spring in Town,* painted by Grant Wood at the end of his life. The scene is the harvest of one's own labor, set on the edge of a small Iowa town. Quilts hang on a laundry line. Two men beat a carpet spread on the grass. A young girl bends the bough of a cherry tree in blossom. The painting is dominated by a broad-backed, shirtless young man turning the soil with a garden fork. He is nearly as large as the white-spired church rising on a hill at the edge of town, and he could have posed as Milo of Crotona. The geometry of his unplanted garden, as well as its tilth, is perfect, altered only by a row of irises. The compost of last year's vegetation has already been spread. The formalism of Versailles — a monarchical, absolutist vision of garden geometry — has been pared down to this democratic, self-reliant vision of gardening.

September

I've looked at this print almost daily for years — I come from a place like this modest town — and only now do I see that there is an ending here too. The year of this painting is 1941. A war is already being fought in Europe. Before this man can choose seeds for next year's garden — a Victory Garden by then — he will be gone, called to war, his annual tilling delayed perhaps forever.

⸺ ⸺ ▰◈▰ ⸺ ⸺

On the first Friday after that sudden Tuesday, I took an afternoon train back homeward out of Manhattan and into the country. Do you remember the day? The clouds were pulling apart in the distance, exposing blue sky along the western horizon. The streets of Harlem took the light and held it, their brick buildings seeming almost to swell with solidity. In the substance of those streets and the surface of the river and the embrace of the railroad bridge into the Bronx, there was a profound, material comfort. "Material" is the important word. The world into which I was passing exuded nothing but its own repose. It had no news to deliver, or rather only the old, inarticulate news that bricks and water and steel have always delivered.

After a while I reached my stop and drove north along a highway through the cornfields. Here too I felt the same thing, that there was a mute voice in the extreme order of those rows of corn, in the rasp of their drying leaves against each other.

The round bales in the hayfields looked like a gathering point for shadows. The trees slipped by dispassionately.

It's often possible to look at a rural landscape and feel that you're being drawn into it, that what you see in the distance somehow tugs you outward along the line of sight. But this was just the opposite. The countryside seemed to pour itself down into the windows of the pickup, the empty corncribs, the neat stacks of firewood, the mellifluous pastures on the highest hillsides. At home the horses and dogs consoled me in a way I couldn't understand, until I finally realized that they could not be told what had happened that week. In that fact lay the consolation. They had only the old news to give, their old satisfaction with the world as they know it.

Life is bearing witness. In some superficial sense the morning of September 11 sifted us all into different circles of witnessing. Some people narrowly escaped the collapsing towers. Others watched in terrified safety from windows and rooftops farther uptown. Many, like me, saw it live on television from midtown, while an incalculable number of people around the country and the world watched as the tapes were replayed into the night and the coming days. But we're all witnesses, no matter what we saw or how we saw it. Our burden is very different from the burden the victims bore and their families still bear, but it's no less real.

Witnessing is a matter of knowledge and of conscience. We know what we saw, and yet we watch the televised tapes play over and over again because we disbelieve what we know. We also watch because it feels as if we're attesting to history, denouncing a crime, renewing a commitment, and also because to break off watching feels like a betrayal. It's hard to know, just yet, whether for each of us this witnessing has caused an erosion or a sedimentation, a stripping away of the skin or a callusing. But paradoxical as it may sound, to continue to bear witness, in conscience, it may be necessary to stop watching for a while, to turn off the television, to break what for some people has become a self-reinforcing circle of despair.

There's no abiding consolation at the moment. But the clouds do sometimes pull apart, if only temporarily. The day after I got home, I stopped by a small lumber mill to pick up some siding that the owner had cut for a chicken house I'm building. It was the sort of day we've been having plenty of, luminous and deep. The owner waved from behind a metal grinder that was throwing off sparks and pointed me toward the mill. On its wooden rails lay my lumber, smooth, fragrant planks of pine, scalloped and grooved to fit together the way so few things seemed to be doing elsewhere. I ran my hand down their lengths, felt the light flouring of sawdust on each board, and for the moment thought of nothing else.

I was in Eads, Colorado, just passing through, which is true of nearly everyone who has ever come to Eads. The town lies on a major truck route across southeastern Colorado. What Eads takes from that truck route is hard to tell. A few people stop now and then at Shepp's drive-in, on the edge of town. Plastic lambs line the windowsills, and you can read a religious magazine called *Guideposts* while you wait for lunch, for the full name of Shepp's is the Good Sheppard Inn.

But only the locals turn off the truck route and onto the main street of Eads. On one side lies the Crow-Luther Arts Center, which used to be the Plains movie theater. Its marquee says, almost ironically, THANK YOU FOR SUPPORTING THE FINE ARTS. One of the E's has blown sideways in the wind.

Across the street and down a little is the Kiowa County Museum, an old-fashioned brick building with a concrete stoop. Inside you can see the optimistic plat that was laid out for Eads many decades ago, a grid of house lots marching off in all directions. You can see a few collections of arrowheads and some old-fashioned kitchen equipment — a couple of pressure cookers and a wood-fired stove. One room is devoted to a frightening display of antiquated medical equipment. There's a room full of cowboy gear and a photograph of the record corn harvest before dust obscured the future of agriculture in Kiowa County. The pathos lies not in the objects themselves but in what you would need to know about the life at hand to give them their real meaning, a knowledge not readily available to passersby.

But on one wall, even a stranger could decipher the whole story. Leaning against the wall was the side panel of a school bus from seventy years ago. Above it hung the receipt the county coroner submitted for mileage costs. There were banner headlines and the photographs of five children. They had boarded a bus after school with fifteen other children on March 26, 1931, in Towner, Colorado, a small town almost on the Kansas line. The bus was caught in deepening snowfall a few miles south of Towner, caught in the kind of spring blizzard that ranchers dread. Some panes of glass were missing in the school bus, and snow drifted in. By the time the children were rescued, at noon two days later, five were dead. The body of the bus driver was found in the open fields, his hands badly lacerated from trying to follow a fence line to summon help.

Farther south of Towner, down in the Arkansas Valley, the snow had fallen as rain. The same was true farther east, in Kansas. But the altitude at Towner, which lies due east of Eads, was just high enough to sustain a blizzard. The country there is as stark as a coroner's receipt, even on a hot autumn day with no chance of snow in it. Or perhaps that's just the way it seems after reading those old headlines and looking into those almost forgotten faces. Their names were Louise Stonebreaker, Bobby Brown, Arlo Unte, Kenneth Johnson, and Mary Louise Miller, the youngest of them all. The bus driver was Mary Louise's father.

◂━ ☰◊☰ ━▸

At halftime in Absarokee, Montana, last Friday night, the candidates for homecoming queen of Absarokee High School stood at midfield, young women shivering in bright, backless gowns as though they were creatures just uncocooned. Beside each queen candidate stood a king candidate who was also a football player with helmet-matted hair, a running back or tight end or linebacker armored in black and orange, the colors of the Absarokee Huskies. The rest of the Huskies had just tramped off the field, and the king candidates looked impatient to follow, detained only by female hands laid lightly upon their arms. The Huskies were trouncing the Lodge Grass Indians, from the Crow Reservation, and the mood was high, for this would be the Huskies' first victory of the season, 42–8.

The Huskies had made all the pregame noises required of football players pumping up for a homecoming game. They groaned and grunted and thumped each other on shoulder pads and helmets. They seemed to be trying these noises on for size, as though they didn't quite believe in the ferocity they showed or weren't quite certain who they were showing it for. The psychological distance from the bleachers to the playing field, even in a small town like Absarokee, is as great as that from the dress circle to a Broadway stage. The players felt it. Even the water boy felt it, running in self-conscious haste to the loose huddle that formed onfield during time-outs.

Rain was expected, and fans had parked directly behind the bleachers in case of it. But the rain held off, and so the pep band played and the cheerleaders cheered and students strolled back and forth along the cinder track in front of the bleachers as if it were a midway of sorts, while on the field a boy named Wilcox was being tackled by a boy named Rides the Bear. Young cowboys walked past riding their hips like horses. Girls walked past in knots of four or five, borrowing babies from the hands of the mothers they passed. Children played in the sand pit where broad-jumpers would land during track season. Everyone felt the season pivoting, as if the giant illuminated *A* on the hill above Absarokee High stood suddenly for Autumn.

━━ ✥ ━━

The weight of the afternoon sun already falls more lightly on my back than it did a few weeks ago. The days seem not only shorter but also somehow thinner too, and every morning that dawns above freezing feels like a morning won back from the inevitable. Nothing is dry yet, of course, but the promise of eventual dryness is in the air. A day will come when every crown of seeds will rattle on the weeds in ditches and fields, when leaves will crunch obligingly underfoot again.

A wet summer is a dark summer, and around here this was one of the darkest summers on record. In fact, darkness was about ten inches above normal by the time fall began. Never were the fungicidal qualities of exterior paint more highly prized than during this summer past. Old wooden barns and outbuildings became studies in parasitism. In our bedroom a mushroom the size of a child's head sprouted from an interior beam. All in all, it was a good summer to be an epiphyte from one of the gloomier, more downcast species.

But as autumn advances, the woods will open up again. The deep shade, which seemed so unfamiliar when it first returned in late spring, will dissipate. Antiseptic sunlight will again reach the waterlogged earth beneath the great stands of oak and maple. Even as daylight slackens week by week, the turning, yellowing leaves will reflect more light in wavelengths with a warm, inviting cast. As the leaves cover the ground, the floor of the deciduous forest will begin to throw light upward toward the sky. The landscape will seem to decrease in volume because the woods are bare.

What all of this means is that the catbird will be leaving soon. It's lived in the green shade beside a rotting porch all summer long. I glimpse it only now and then — a slender gray bird wearing a black skullcap, scratching among the lower branches along the edge of the woods. When it calls, it doesn't sound like a cat meowing. It sounds like an imitation of a cat meowing, like a squirrel throwing its voice in order to puzzle a dog. But when it sings, the catbird distills shadows into music, the way the nightingale does in English poetry. There's a faintly mechanical quality to its song, as though the notes were produced by small bells or the operation of intricate machinery. When the woods open up and there's no shade left to hide it, the catbird will go. Summer will finally have come to an end.

The farmers I buy hay from said it wasn't frost the other morning. I saw them walking across high, rocky ground, beyond a barbed-wire fence and an old truck body, driving heifers from one pasture into another. Each man carried an old, smooth stick with a wide crook in the end. The older farmer walked as though he hated cattle — would like for just one morning to sleep in and not have to wonder what spooked the cows through the fence during the night. He was hunched, sore from what might be Lyme disease or what he calls "sugar" — meaning diabetes — or just lingering stiffness from the ribs he broke when he fell from a hay wagon in June. He looked cold, as if the frost had gotten into him.

Except that it wasn't frost, just heavy dew. The roof on that dairy barn had turned white, and on my deck at home the wood was grease-slick. But the thermometer had only read thirty-six degrees overnight. All the cold air had slid downhill into a basin of fog. From my place I could see its limbs, and from the hillside where those two farmers work, I could see the body of the fog slowly dissolving down in the hollow on what would turn out to be a bright fall day, the first day that truly felt like fall. Where moths had tented the tree limbs along the road, it looked as though the fog had torn off in rough shreds as it shouldered downhill toward town.

I had driven across the valley at seven-thirty and up onto the skyline farm for a load of hay, the fifth or sixth in a week of fourteen-mile round trips for hay. We'll stack eight hundred bales in our barn by the time we're done, and the pickup holds fifty-two bales. Sometimes both farmers stack hay in the truck, and sometimes I take the place of one and climb onto the hay wagon and toss bales down. The running gear creaks as I work my way, kneeling, across the top row of bales. I can smell the smoke from the woodstove that burns year-round in the milk room across the barnyard. The emergency-services radio in the coveralls of one of the farmers scratches out an unintelligible phrase from time to time. How an actual emergency sounds is hard to tell. Perhaps the pitch is higher or the unintelligible words run closer together.

At home I ease an orange hay elevator onto the stack in the pickup. It starts with a whine that never lets up, kicking loose hay into the air, throwing dust into the sunlight. The bales catch on the chain-teeth and shudder upward at an angle into the darkness of the mow, where my wife's hands and my father's hands catch them. The horses stand by the barnyard gate and watch philosophically, deeply satisfied with the proceedings. The barn dog lies by the horse trailer and watches too. His house is filled with last year's hay, swept down from the mow when we began stacking a few days ago. We're all bone tired. Real frost will come tonight, and it will bring down the garden, which was doing a good job of bringing itself down already. We should stack wood or lift tomato cages or till ground for next year's garlic. Instead we'll sit in the autumn sunshine and enjoy being bone tired, harvesting our fatigue.

October

The weather has been unseasonably hot in central Iowa, and farmers who are used to worrying about getting crops out of the fields before the weather turns wintry are harvesting with the air-conditioning turned up full in the cabs of their combines. The Midwest is never more beautiful than at this season, even though the air is dull with humidity. The ditches have ripened into pale ocherous colors, shades of russet intermixed, and in the fields where soybeans have already been harvested, the stubble lies slicked back like an old man's crew cut. The corn hasn't stood in shocks for sixty years and more, but even as it stands — still in rows, dry, skeletal ruins of the plant it was in mid-August — it suggests cool weather, sharp nights, and the plumage of that most autumnal bird, the pheasant.

Because of the dry, warm weather, harvest is running ahead of schedule, and the fields are full of machinery. All-devouring combines run down the rows cutting twenty-foot swaths well into the night, moving across the landscape in the darkness, their lights suggesting earthgoing yachts or mobile oil refineries. Grain wagons pull alongside, offloading beans or corn from the combines' hoppers. In the stubble rows, trucks with red boxes wait to be loaded, and then one after another they make their way to grain elevators and storage bins, where grain dryers work ceaselessly. The local news programs report uneven crop maturity, and when they're asked, farmers say they hope for a freeze.

It's a laborious landscape, and that's part of its beauty. But even as farmers stare ahead at the rows of uncut corn in the headlights, their minds are on the grain glut, which has dropped prices below the cost of production, and on the decline in the value of farmland. The fields are enormous, the yields are remarkable, the machinery is gargantuan, and so is the level of agricultural debt. The margin on which the enterprise operates this year is nearly nonexistent, which is why, as farmers watch the harvest progress, their minds are also on Washington, where year after year Democrats and Republicans debate the terms of relief.

October

One day last spring the fire in the kitchen woodstove went out and was never relit. I didn't record the date, because some endings are lost in a crowd of beginnings, passing unnoticed until months later, when the oversight seems almost melancholy. So I note here the first fire of the new season: October 4, thermometer lodged in the midforties, a chill in the bones of the house, rain falling hard through dwindling yellow hickory leaves. When the kindling caught the first dry log — a length of honey locust — in its flames, the stove called all the dogs. They sprawled across the warm tiles, mouths agape. Not a half hour had ticked away, and there we were, back on the night before the fire went out for the last time last spring.

A kind of accounting has been going on here for the past few weeks, how many pounds of honey gathered, how many bales of hay laid up in the loft, how many cords of wood stacked and under cover. This is such an ancestral satisfaction — the antithesis of the city's constant abundance — that it feels almost embarrassing to acknowledge it, the sign of the hayseed. The manure pile, steaming in the cool drizzle, looks like simple wealth, and so do the hickory nuts that crack beneath my feet as I walk to the barn and the milkweed pods that crowd against the fence line, ready to burst. The mice are fattening up in the woodshed. There's a fine crop of horsehair coming in on the mares and the gelding. It will go to make bird nests in spring.

In April what you see are your own intentions. In October you see their unexpected wreck and fulfillment. All summer potato vines spread across a corner of the garden. But when I lifted a plant, hoping to rob new potatoes, I saw that the vines, every one, had rotted right at the soil. Meanwhile two peach trees — planted vainly, I thought, by previous owners — blossomed heavily and set fruit. When September came, the peaches turned as red as the Virginia creeper is turning now. I finally picked one, just to savor my doubts. But it was the very promise of a peach. A garden is so full of cheap sermons.

◆━◆ ⇥◆⇤ ◆━◆

I found myself Monday on a stretch of rural highway in eastern Colorado at the time of morning when round bales lying in the hay fields look like cattle grazing, and vice versa. I was driving toward the sunrise, which was still only a premonition in the distance. The horizon in that direction was a long, low ridgeline dotted either with trees that resembled a band of clouds or clouds that had rooted themselves with stems to earth or possibly very large sheep moving single file with a grim and stately purpose.

Over the ridge and into the next swale rode the pickup, and there I saw a small corral with four horses, all of them looking intently — wishfully, I suspect — at the kitchen light that had just been switched on in a dark ranch house across the barnyard. On a fence post near the road sat a bulbous red-tailed hawk. The rising light caught in his eye, and to me he looked dour, hungry for a diet less rich in rodents, a palate-cleansing carrot perhaps or a plate of watercress.

I've always loved the crescendo Monday brings, but I've always thought of it in strictly urban terms. By the time darkness has begun to wear away on a New York Monday morning, the city has rumbled to life, shaking off Sunday like a distant childhood. Soon the streets are filled with people, some of whom look as though their coattails had caught in the city's gears and dragged them headlong from their beds. Millions of weekday morning habits iterate themselves anew, yet even the familiarity of it all seems somehow fresh.

But in deep country, near, say, Last Chance, Colorado, the week evolves more slowly. Monday's chores look much like Sunday's. The headlong rush to get kids off to school is no different on the Colorado plains than anywhere else. But once the school bus has come and gone, once the high school kids have driven themselves off to class in a neighboring town, silence falls over the highway again. The low angle of the sun seems to give every object it strikes a higher profile. Its light throws the long shadow of a pickup and horse trailer into the far ditch, where the driver waves to himself.

On yet another fence post another hawk preens, and on the unplowed side of the road antelope move stiffly up a ridge and out of sight. Then the highway is still, except for the wind. What day of the week it is is anybody's guess until the next vehicle passes, when, for a moment — in the presence of a service truck or a postal carrier or a delivery van — Monday reappears.

When fall comes to the Southwest, the chamisa blooms, and suddenly a shrub that is inconspicuous most of the year seems to dominate the landscape. An old chamisa plant grows upright out of a weir of downswept dead boughs, and its whiplike pale green branches terminate in clumps of yellow florets, which brush against one's hips. When rain falls — and Santa Fe recently got half an inch — the scent of chamisa seems almost too heavy for the wind to carry. The odor is opaque, insidious. It infiltrates. It loiters. Even with nostrils buried deep in the plant, you end up asking, What does chamisa smell like?

The common name of chamisa is rabbitbrush, and the scientific name is *Chrysothamnus nauseosus,* which says something about the olfactory impression chamisa makes on botanists. But *nauseosus* is a pretty vague descriptor. If you went about giving binomial names to the artifacts of modern life, how many of them might deserve *nauseosus* as their specific term? Coming upon a stand of chamisa, trying again to decipher its scent, you wonder, *Nauseosus* how? "It smells like a rank little fox," said one Santa Fe resident. "It smells like being four years old," said another, an answer that hints at the profound association between odor and memory. To use the perfumer's language, the scent of chamisa is at once woody, green, and animalic, with several miscellaneous notes thrown in. It smells like a kitchen full of fresh herbs where a mouse has died behind the stove. It smells like a sachet in a drawer full of rubber gloves. It smells like the Southwest in autumn.

October

Talking about scent is like speaking a foreign tongue badly: you're always searching for a word that lies just out of reach, uncertain, finally, of your own meaning. It's easier to describe a complex emotion than a complex odor. What do the dogs of Santa Fe think when the chamisa comes into bloom? Perhaps an entire spectrum of scent goes into eclipse, concealed beneath the weight of rabbitbrush. Or perhaps in the unending orchestration of smell in their world, the blossoming of chamisa is like the sudden entrance of the cello section, playing slightly out of tune and out of tempo. In the end, you're brought up hard against the circularity of scent. Chamisa smells like chamisa. And vice versa.

On a warm October afternoon, high in a sugar maple, a crow tore apart a hornet's nest, discarding shreds of gray hornet-paper like leaves in a monochrome fall. A hail of ladybugs rose and then fell against the south side of the house. They were hapless fliers burdened by ungainly wing-covers, clattering almost inaudibly against the parched siding, seeking cracks and lifted clapboards to winter under. The sight of so many ladybugs in flight, each one armed with a faint acrid stench, looked like the threat of a hard season coming. When that many creatures take shelter at once, you wonder what they're sheltering from. Soon we'll know.

The woods are bright, brighter where the maples stand

175

against a backdrop of unchanging hemlock. Even as light leaks out of the month, the woods seem to compensate, opening again to the western horizon. The sun has made its way southward like the fox that crosses the pasture most evenings. The air wears the tannic acidity of decaying leaves. The suppleness of light just when it fades in late afternoon seems almost mocking. It's a humiliating display of color, towering out of the treetops and into the backlit clouds overhead. At twilight Lindy found a newly killed male cardinal lying in the grass, its head severed by one of our cats. There was nothing in the day as sharply defined as the line where the black around its bill met the red of its crest.

That morning I had lit a brush pile on fire. There was a raucous half hour when the flames seemed to catch at something inside me. Then the fire settled down to business, smoldering steadily, adding its own taint to the air. Crab apple leaves on boughs cut a day earlier shriveled like a time-lapse glimpse of late autumn. The fruit sizzled and dropped into the flames. A couple of hours later the pile was nothing more than a small mound of ash.

After twilight had come and gone and the temperature had dropped, I walked down again to where the bonfire had been. I turned the ashes with a manure fork. A night breeze blew across the coals and reddened them. They seemed to ripple in the darkness, their light refracted by their heat. For a moment I stood beside them, taking in their warmth. The unsteady lights in the ashes looked like the fires of some ancient city seen from high above, a place described by Goethe long ago, when he

October

wrote, "The king is out hunting, the queen is expecting a child, and so things could not be better."

⋯⋯ ☲◈☲ ⋯⋯

At noon today, local apparent sidereal time will be approximately 1:29. The Julian Day will be 2450384, which is the number of days since high noon on the first of January 4713 B.C.E. That was the last time the twenty-eight-year solar and nineteen-year lunar cycles began on the same day as a fifteen-year Roman tax cycle, a coincidence first noticed in 1582 by the percipient Joseph Justus Scaliger, who invented the Julian calendar. Exactly 7,980 years will have passed before these cycles resume in unison and a new Julian Period begins, in the year 3267. (*That* will be some celebration.) If you probe a little deeper into the subject of time, you discover leap seconds and negative leap seconds and International Seconds. There's a Modified Julian Date and a Truncated Julian Date. There are ideal clocks generating proper time. Greenwich Mean Time has a familiar, prime meridian ring to it, but alas it's been replaced by Coordinated Universal Time, which sounds as though Earth presumed to control the clockwork in the distant cosmos.

But what do we call the hour we gained when we set our clocks back last night? It has no name. You make a pilgrimage to all the appliances — the alarm clocks, the wall clocks, the coffeemaker, the telephone, the VCR, the PC — and it seems

177

for a moment as though time were a utility that got pumped into the house with the alternating current. Daylight Saving Time is the ultimate flat tax. Everybody pays up when it begins on the first Sunday in April, and on the last Sunday in October everybody reaps a one hundred percent refund of their hour, not a second of it lost to overhead. There are a few confusing exceptions. The Hopi Reservation doesn't observe Daylight Saving Time. The Navajo Nation, which surrounds the Hopi Reservation, does. The state of Arizona, which surrounds Navajos and Hopis alike, doesn't. All three entities returned to synchronicity with the rest of the country, and their neighbors, last night. So did Indiana.

There's a geographical equivalent to this temporal leap. Imagine driving north through the open prairie, along the edge of one township after another. (A township is a surveyed square six miles to a side.) The farther north you go, the more the lines of longitude converge, which means the township grid is steadily being compressed by the longitudinal grid. To adjust for this, the road north makes a lateral jog every twenty-four miles. We have just made the big jog east (the sun rises earlier now) on the northward road into winter. We keep going this direction for another fifty-five days until the road ends and the tundra begins. Out there the caribou and musk ox are grazing, a sign that it will be time to turn around and head back south toward summer.

W hen snow began falling on Sunday, I realized that a line from Keats — "until they think warm days will never cease" — had been running through my head for weeks. The line is from "To Autumn," one of the loveliest poems in the language, and "they" are the bees, whose "clammy cells," as Keats calls their comb, have been "o'erbrimm'd" by summer. Jonathan Bate, author of a book called *The Song of the Earth,* observes that the late summer of 1819, the season leading up to the completion of Keats's ode on September 19, "was clear and sunny on thirty-eight out of the forty-seven days from 7 August to 22 September" and that temperatures were milder in the final week of that period than they had been in three years.

This wasn't merely a spate of beautiful weather. It was weather of a kind, Bate notes, that would actually make breath come easier for a consumptive like Keats. There could be nothing more personal than the question of Keats's lung capacity, and yet "To Autumn" doesn't read as a personal poem. There's something deceptively long-winded in the syntax of the first stanza, and some critics have seen a consumptive's hectic flush in the stubble plains touched with "rosy hue." But Bate reminds us, too, how broad the boundaries of "personal" experience really are. For Keats those boundaries include the season as a whole. The fine weather o'erbrimm'd him, and in doing so gave voice to itself.

Until the past few days, it was a Keatsian autumn, full of what the poet calls, in a letter from those same weeks, "chaste weather — Dian skies." Never mind that the leaves are now almost gone, or that the skies are now unchaste, gray, and dousing us with snow showers. Somehow the brightness of the trees created the illusion that the periphery of my awareness had expanded. When Lindy and I walked the dogs, it felt as though we were all walking with eyebrows raised, though for the dogs that would be with nostrils distended.

Keats personified autumn, imagining her by a cider press or fast asleep in a "half-reap'd furrow." Personifying the natural world is so fundamental and so limitless that it seems sometimes like the foundation of all poetry. To some, I suppose, personifying nature is an act of hubris, a refusal to accept the otherness of the world around us. But in a fall like this one — dry after a long wet, warm after unusual coolness — personifying nature seems like a means of meeting nature halfway. In the ghostliness of Keats's autumn, "sitting careless on a granary floor," what we really see is the way the season swells within us.

November

For some reason, every stage in this advancing season has brought with it a feeling of incredulity. A few weeks ago it seemed unbelievable that the leaves should be turning so soon and then that they should have dropped so promptly. Now, just this week, it seems incredible that snow should have fallen out of a goose-gray sky, skidding eastward toward the missing sun. I wake up thinking, "November already," and realize that "already" is a word that's been with me all autumn long, always measuring how far behind the season I feel.

The weather has been anything but harsh. Even the few frosts so far have been less than militant. But I seem to be holding back, feeling a reluctance about winter I've never felt before. Usually there's something purely pragmatic about that feeling, a long list of jobs that still need doing, most of them the kind whose only satisfaction is knowing they're done. Nearly everyone who lives in the country feels crowded for time right now. "Racing daylight" is the phrase I hear, and I hear it from men and women who've been racing daylight, working outdoors this time of year, their whole lives. There's something different in the way they say it now. You hear hesitation from the most unhesitant people.

It takes no imagination to stay synchronized with the shifting of the season, with the retracting daylight or the sudden gathering of a wet morning wind that gets behind your ears and under your hair when you feed the animals. You don't really even have to pay attention to keep up with the calendar. But you do have to be ready to part with the days that have already passed. September took far more than a month this year. It probably took two months, the one our bodies lived and the wholly different month we lived in our minds. Time fell out of gear for almost everyone.

Some of the reluctance that comes with this autumn is mere uncertainty, a sense that no one really knows the score. Going into winter takes confidence, even in a normal year, even if it's nothing more than confidence in one's own preparations. Somehow that's not good enough this year. Like everyone, I find myself wanting the world to be right with itself again, even if only in the wrong old ways. In the heart of the reluctance I feel and hear in the voices of my neighbors, there's a longing for the inconsequential summer we were having not so many weeks ago. Longing is probably too strong a word. Better to say that the memory of what was, for many Americans, an uneventful August exerts a certain attraction right now. But the present is irrefutable. The leaves won't rise again, except on a cold wind. Before long, I hope, that won't seem so regrettable.

—◆—✠◆✠—◆—

The last of the World War I veterans are almost impossibly old by now. They flicker past in the war footage shown repeatedly on late-night television, young men burdened by the weight of arms, with everything that implies. Now nearly all those men are dead, and the few still living seem to symbolize the enormous changes that have swept across the world in the years since the armistice was signed in 1918. In the presence of men and women of advanced age, it's always tempting to behave like the host of the postmodern world, welcoming them to life as we know it, inviting them to marvel at the place we've all wound up, bristling as it does with the latest technology. The roles should be reversed. The old ones should be hosting us, inviting us to contemplate with them the intractable knowledge that comes from a place like the battlefields of World War I, where every faith — and especially the faith in moral and technical advancement — seemed to totter.

The armistice was signed in November, the eleventh hour of

the eleventh day of the eleventh month. On its own, November can be bleak enough. The leaves are gone, and the trees seem frayed. A ridgeline of blackened, upthrust boughs seems to mirror the rain. The clouds have the texture of steel wool. Winter could come the next minute or the next month. But what November has ever been like November in the embattled salients of the Great War, where the earth itself was dismembered and interred, its flesh confused with the flesh of soldiers, horses, and mules? Even at peace, nature seems disordered, almost skeletal, in November. The consolation lies in the woodsmoke spiraling out of chimneys, the light in windows as the day goes down. It lies in the unbroken rhythm of living at peace, where the hour of armistice — the end of that painful caesura — is almost forgotten.

Lindy and I moved into this house on November 13, a day, that first year, with thirteen hours of freezing rain. In the years since, a part of me has been grafted onto this place, and I'm still waiting to learn whether it's a vital part or not. I promised when we bought this house — Lindy recalls this clearly — to take things slowly, to bring about changes at a leisurely pace. I thought of that promise recently as I stood atop a stepladder in the kitchen, whacking the fireplace with a sledgehammer while Lindy tried to catch the dust before it landed. Our property abounds in firewood, and it had occurred to us that a freestanding wood-stove would be more practical than the largely useless fireplace taking up a corner of the kitchen. We opened a wall in a mildly interrogative manner. Once we did, we could see that the fireplace was just a sheet-metal firebox set behind a cheap façade of cement-board, mortar, and unattractive stone of a kind you might use to make mountains in a model railroad.

It all came down one Saturday morning, opening up what had been a narrow doorway between the kitchen and dining room and revealing a beautiful old beam. An old-house owner is a prospector, staking his claim on worn linoleum, tattered wallpaper, or painted wallboard. The hope is that beneath them lies an undefiled treasure of architectural detail or sumptuous wood, which a previous generation of owners — sick of looking at refined carpentry and the grain of chestnut or oak — covered with horrors all their own. The hope is often satisfied, but not often unambiguously. The beam we revealed is hand-hewn and completely sound except for the last foot on its eastern end. That will take some fudging. As we poke at this building, we discover in its bones the effects of lifelong bad posture, occasional inadequacies in the diet, and the signs of one or two serious accidents that would have killed a lesser domicile.

By now I find myself living in a house that barely resembles the one I thought we were buying. The house has changed us more than we've changed it. I almost never smack my head on the low ceiling over the stairs to the mudroom anymore. For me that passage has grown taller over the past year. Visitors smack their heads again and again, no matter how often I warn them, which confirms that the ceiling is just where it was when we moved in. And though Lindy and I have begun to wear a comforting groove into this place, much like the one the horses have worn through the barnyard, our daydreams grow more and more elaborate. Every day we're surrounded by the adaptations other people have made to what was once, long ago, a simple rectangular structure, scarcely more than a wood-frame cabin on a hillside. Two centuries of change are telescoped into our day-to-day experience.

In nearly every way, it would be easier to alter a new house to our needs. But there's something static about a new house, something terminal. This old house invites adaptation because it embodies a history of adaptation. A new house just stands there, settling, waiting for someone to come along and wonder what's under those walls or why two bedrooms can't be merged into one.

So this is where time has led us. The kitchen deck must go. It slopes toward the house and gets about ten minutes of sunlight on midwinter afternoons. In late November a glacier begins to build in that dark, antarctic corner, and it only ceases calving icebergs into the azalea bed about the end of April. To replace the deck — someday — we have in mind a stone terrace sheltered by a pergola, a pergola knotted with climbing hydrangea or a hops plant or, since we're daydreaming, ceanothus. Lindy's workroom — a small, crazed addition — must go as well. Its foundation is cracked, and its eaves actually cut across the lower corners of two windows upstairs.

Besides the days when we fret about our plans for this house, there are also days that approach perfection, when things seem fine just as they are. This was an autumn full of those days, the kind that lull you into believing that winter will never come, or that when it does come it will bring only snowfall or blue skies, not thirteen hours of freezing rain. The sugar maples turned, and the goldenrod blazed all around us. I poked around at the base of a compost heap I started in April and found that time had turned a pile of horse manure, waste straw, weeds, and grass clippings into friable compost. I took a cart of it up to the asparagus bed and mulched it heavily. I buried the feet of all the roses in fresh manure and cut down the peonies. Then I walked to the high end of the pasture, above the maples, and looked back at the house, itself almost the color of goldenrod. I imagined that I could see smoke from the new woodstove, which still lay crated in the barn, drifting out of the chimney and beyond it the first flakes of snow against the distant hills.

Aldo Leopold's ecological testament, *A Sand County Almanac*, was a posthumous book, appearing a year and a half after Leopold died of a heart attack in April 1948 at the age of sixty-one. A graduate of the Yale Forestry School and a seventeen-year veteran of the U.S. Forest Service, Leopold had his greatest influence, during his lifetime, as a professor of game management at the University of Wisconsin. But it's the *Almanac*, his meditations on a Wisconsin River farm and an unequivocal statement of conscience, that will carry his influence and his good name down the generations.

Leopold's extraordinary contribution to our world was to articulate the idea of a land ethic. The human relation to land, he wrote, "is still strictly economic, entailing privileges but not obligations." Leopold believed that the basis of successful conservation was to extend to nature the ethical sense of responsibility that humans extend to each other. This idea has acquired tremendous force since *A Sand County Almanac* first appeared. The fact that the idea now seems unexceptionable is a measure of its widespread influence.

Fifty years is both a very short and a very long time in the life of a good idea. The power of Leopold's argument — buttressed as it is by his clear, vigorous prose — has not been blunted in the least. In fact his argument seems more urgently true now than ever. In the past fifty years Leopold's work has helped drive the environmental movement. Yet the tendencies he lamented, summed up in the phrase "despoliation of land," have accelerated almost out of control.

Leopold will last not because he captured a moment or a feeling, though he does both in the first sections of *A Sand County Almanac*. He will last because we have scarcely begun to work out the implications of his ideas. He suggested an "ecological interpretation of history," which has only recently begun to be written. He recognized that the "ability to see the cultural value of wilderness boils down . . . to a question of intellectual humility." He described a dynamic that still threatens wildness. "The very scarcity of wild places, reacting with the mores of advertising and promotion," he wrote, "tends to defeat any deliberate effort to prevent their growing still more scarce."

These are formidable ideas. But none are more challenging than Leopold's land ethic. It requires a rerooting in nature, a forsaking of the hope that we can save wild or even open land on the basis of its economic value. We are busy, Leopold says, "inventing subterfuges to give [nature] economic importance." They won't work. There's a risk involved in creating a truly ethical relation to the land. But Leopold believed in risk. "Too much safety," he wrote, "seems to yield only danger in the long run."

—————

I suppose that if I were a woolly bear caterpillar or a squirrel storing hickory nuts or one of the other creatures said to know in advance the severity of the winter ahead, I would be able to do just the right amount of work to get ready for it. Instead I have to prepare for winter in the subjunctive, as if it were going to be severe — as if I were a doomsaying squirrel. Like most people, I'm not a very good student of my own behavior, but I've noticed in myself an urge these days to get ready for winter. I noticed it because it led me down to the barn one morning and kept me hard at work for several days, stacking hay in the loft, preparing to heat the horses' water tank, making a place in the barn aisle where the horseshoer could work under lights and out of the wind.

On a warm noon when sun strikes the hive, the bees still fly, but it's been cold enough recently for them to form their winter cluster, a tight, buzzing ball at the center of their store of brood and honey. The flow of information into the hive — and with it nectar and pollen — has dwindled to nothing. In fields and waste places, the stands of goldenrod, the source of the late-summer honey flow, have turned a nebulous silver, like wool caught on barbed wire. I took a few frames of honey for the house but left most of it for the bees because it's a new hive and, again, because I have no way of knowing how bad this winter will get.

At dusk I stand in the door of the hayloft and look out over the place, at the ridgeline newly visible behind a copse of birches to the west, at the row of denuded sugar maples that ring the pasture. The moon has already risen into a bank of thin clouds that look tinged by firelight, clouds the color of the dogwood leaves. The horses in the barnyard below me show the whites of their eyes while dismantling a hay bale. They've been slow to hair up for the season, but now their coats are coming on strong. On the way to the house, I notice that the leaves on the peach trees haven't turned. They're still the green of mid-summer. Is this an omen? Will this be a balmy winter after all? Or does it mean I should provision the larder — a phrase with a satisfying sound — for the snowbound weeks ahead? I just don't know.

November

This time of year the light is always coming and going. Dawn swells until noon, and then, after a brief hesitation, twilight takes over. The sun edges around the day like a fox making homeward tracks along the margin of a snow-covered field. Summer, in memory, seems almost like a plain of sunshine, without undulation. There's an astronomical explanation for it all — the sun cuts a much lower angle across the sky in late autumn and sets farther south. But it's simpler to say that at this time of year, in the country at least, emotion and light are one and the same.

This is never truer than on a dark November morning well before sunrise. A few days ago a freezing rain fell. The day began with the clatter of ice pellets against the windows. It sounded like crows dancing on the skylight. The falling ice was colorless, almost invisible against the thicket of bare woods. But by evening the freezing rain had turned to snow, and before long six inches had fallen over a glaze of ice.

By early Monday morning the balance of light had changed completely. All the dark, difficult textures of earth — the matted bogs, the serrated fields — had been smoothed over, simplified. What seemed before to entangle the light now reflected it. Even at five-thirty on an overcast morning the snow seemed to phosphoresce, to reveal the broad contours of the landscape while concealing its subtlest variations. Even in darkness, driving south, I could sense the snowlit dimension of the long north-south corridors of Columbia County.

In the valley that Route 22 follows, each light seemed to weigh in with a different mood. Halogen lamps on a weekend estate picked out every wrinkle in their field of view. The kitchen windows of a farmhouse burned with an old-fashioned, amber glow. Beyond the farmhouse shone a long bank of lights — the windows of a milking parlor filled with cows grazing at their stanchions, the hiss of the milking machines almost audible in the silence outside, where the barn threw its light on the snow.

—◆—

Our neighbors across the road had to put their dog down a couple of weeks ago. Her name was Molly, and the X rays gave her no hope. For as long as we've lived here, Molly and her owners drove the half mile from their house up the highway and onto our gravel road to feed their horses. Molly rode in the back of the pickup and barked the whole way, coming and going, setting our dogs off every afternoon. Molly was a gong sounding day after day, tipping us toward evening. Our dogs would begin to clamor for dinner — sharp stares, deep sighs, contagious grins — and once it was time for their dinner, it was time to feed the horses and the cats and then, eventually, ourselves.

Days in the country can seem formless this time of year. The day's only shape comes from the light and the weather.

November

The rest is self-discipline, willing yourself to work, willing yourself outdoors into the cold and, increasingly, the darkness. It
took a while up here before I could walk down to the barn at
night without feeling my skin prickle. At those moments I knew
what it felt like to be one of our horses, who take sudden frights
in the daytime just for the fun of it. The nearest predator is a
birch tree hanging over the barnyard, but the horses always
believe the worst. I've learned to trust them entirely at night.
Their stolidity reassures me now when I walk down to the barn
in the blackness. They shift quietly from one foot to another,
ease in and out of the run-in shed. They remind me that everything is just as I left it in the light.

When I went out the door last night, it was snowing hard in
full darkness, and I was late. The horses were still in the pasture,
trying to stand in each other's wind-shadow. They followed me
down to the barn and settled around their hay feeder like a
foursome returning to a long-standing game of bridge. Badger,
the barn dog, watched us from his kennel. I let him out and we
walked up onto the hill that overlooks the barn, the bare maples
in silhouette against the barn lights and the falling snow.
Another light burned near the pasture gate, and snow seemed
to fall only around the edges of the bright globe the lamp cast
into the darkness.

Why Badger lives at the barn is another story, a long one.
He's a big dog, half Airedale, half Australian shepherd, and the
stream of life flows right through him. When I'm with him I feel
like a tributary of that stream. We tromped around in the darkness, the grass crusting with frost and yet softening with snow.

This morning we walked up the road and investigated every overnight track. With new snow on the ground, it was as though I could see, for once, what Badger was smelling. He swiveled along the trail of the big fox who lives near here until we cut across a set of deer tracks making for a break in the fence. Once or twice a hunter's gun went off in the distance. We got home before the sun rose.

———— ≍◊≍ ————

To judge by house and yard decorations in the country, Halloween has spilled over its banks and washed away all of October and much of November. In cities the Christmas season as we know it now — an economic indicator with colored lights and eggnog — can no longer be confined, as it used to be, within the month that begins on the day after Thanksgiving. But Thanksgiving sticks strictly to its allotted Thursday, and the power of this quiet holiday is evident in the trouble so many of us go through to get home in time to honor it. There's something touching about a feast of thanks at which we all find our own reasons to be thankful, in which the feeling is named but not the cause.

The year is getting old and the light weak by the time Thanksgiving comes. The only color in the woods is the green of damp moss and the bright orange berries of bittersweet. There are historic reasons why Thanksgiving falls when it does — matters of Pilgrim fact and presidential proclamation — but over time it's become the holiday that defines this bare season. By the end of the eleventh month, the year is ancient enough to have shown us its wisdom. We know what to be grateful for by now, or gratitude is simply beyond us.

You don't have to be very old to remember Thanksgivings that began at four or five in the morning, when women rose alone in the dark to start cooking the turkey. By the time the men and children got out of bed, the bird had already been roasting for a couple of hours on the back porch in its own enameled turkey roaster, a device that lived in the basement all but one day a year, resembled an electric bassinet, and kept the main oven free for pies. Thanksgiving then meant haste in the early hours, a long delay before the big midafternoon dinner, and scratch meals — why eat now? — for breakfast and lunch, a day in which you went straight from starvation to stupefaction, in which men and children felt more than ordinarily useless whenever they came near the kitchen.

Sitting down to the big meal seems like the crux of Thanksgiving, but it really comes a couple of hours later. The pumpkin pie is gone, the dishes are done, the dogs and overnight guests are napping, and there's a strange vacancy in the afternoon light. For a moment the year halts, a moment when the wakeful aren't quite sure what to do with themselves. In that instant, that hollow in time, you find yourself listening to the unnatural stillness of the afternoon, pausing to look closely at the world around you. That's all the celebration necessary on this most modest, most poignant of days.

December

In late August what snow remains along the ridgelines of the Madison Range, in southwestern Montana, is as gray as a cast antler, and it has the porosity of cruelly weathered bone, almost eaten away by sun and wind and age. Still it's hard not to think of those snowfields as the nucleus from which winter will come, spreading downward in the night, taking the unprepared unawares and bestowing a kind of small-town smugness on those who got their snowblowers tuned up in July. Seasonal morals — think of the grasshopper and the ant — echo down through folk literature, through the commonplaces of our tongue, but no season carries a sterner moral than winter, and what makes it so is snow.

Some people love waking to the sight of new snow. Fallen snow is fine, but I like the sight of it falling, fine as dust or so fat you can hear it land against the kitchen window. I like the tunnel of dry snow you drive through at night, the headlights blanking out a few yards ahead, and the feeling that you're driving into some abyssal vacuum. I like the ground-blizzards and the snow that slithers down the road ahead of you. What I like is the visual impairment snow brings with it, the way it obscures some things and defines others, like the wind.

My grandmother Carley always used to say to me, when I was in one of my childhood snow reveries, "You won't feel that way when you're my age." I'm halfway there now, and nothing's changed. I suppose someday I'll feel tyrannized by snow, but the truest and the most consistent of all the feelings I've ever felt is the one I feel when I look up on a gray day in early December and see that out the window the air has filled with snow, snow as still, as hesitant, as the motes of dust in a morning sunbeam.

It reminds me of a classroom in an old brick school building in Osage, Iowa. There was only one small window, mounted high on the wall near the top of a set of stairs that led down to a dank gymnasium. Through that high window I could see the boughs of some conifer, a Scotch pine or a Norway spruce. Whenever snow begins to fall, wherever I am, I'm in that schoolroom again, watching the flakes balanced in the air against the dark green boughs, waiting for them to thicken and for the wind to multiply them until the snow is so thick that the tree fades from sight, and we're sent home early. The snow fills in our tracks so swiftly that it's doubtful we'll ever find our way back to school, not tomorrow or the day after or for weeks to come.

⊷ ⊷ ☵◆☲ ⊶ ⊶

The urge to quarter the year into seasons is nearly irresistible, whether the impulse is astronomical, agricultural, liturgical, or fiscal. Instead of inhabiting the undivided plain of time, humans prefer to live in the rooms the seasons make, and nearly everyone loves to be reminded of that fact. There's something gratifying about seeing fall, winter, spring, and summer, the very idea of seasonality, represented, no matter how — in a Herrick poem or a Boucher painting or in the stiff vellum pages of a medieval illuminated manuscript. The pleasure of it is so strong that it must be adaptive, a way of preparing a biological affinity in us for what the calendar inevitably holds in store.

But portraits of the seasons give a tight, iconic view of nature. Winter doesn't howl into the last stanza of Keats's autumn, stunning the gnats and swallows, nor does it frostbite the naked toes of Botticelli's vernal nymphs. Reality is less discrete. There isn't a secular hymn to a day of unseasonable warmth on the cusp of winter shortly after heavy rain in an otherwise dry autumn, though days like that do come along. The only season Boucher never painted was the one called mud. We live in fact in a world of margins — every hour an occasion of its own — where sometimes the weather and the landscape and the state of the foliage live up to the idea of the very season we say is at hand.

Like most people I've been waiting for the big arctic blow to begin — a dark whistling high in the treetops — and while waiting I've been visiting the plants that surround the house. They divide into two camps. Some insist on fall and winter, like buckthorn, hung with nearly black berries, and eastern wahoo, a tree whose small, lobed fruits are a mordant pink. But most of the plants I stopped to quiz — climbing roses, elderberry, lilacs, azaleas, rhododendron, blueberries, wisteria, a lone magnolia — are looking patiently toward spring. Dormant buds, covered in bud scales, have already formed in axils and on twigs.

I had always thought of this time of year as a slow patch of death, of stasis at least, in the plant world. That's the sort of thing you believe when you take the idea of season too literally. The mild fall weather may have swollen the buds a little more than usual, but what it really did was drive me outdoors to notice them. There, at the end of autumn, stood the whole shape of spring, held back only by the still-dwindling daylight, by a keen, continuous apprehension of time.

Up past Pipestone, Minnesota, Highway 23 angles away to the north-northeast, through Lyon, Yellow Medicine, and Chippewa Counties, and through the heart of what for twelve years in the mid-nineteenth century was the Dakota Reservation and before that the Dakota homeland. The last time I was there, it had snowed a couple of days earlier, and the highway was a patchwork of dry pavement and hard, rutted ice, where drifting snow had blown across the asphalt in a warm southern wind and frozen overnight. But now the wind was changing. Second by second the balance of brightness shifted back and forth between the overcast sky and the snow-glazed earth, like flakes of mica mirroring each other.

I had flown over this country two days earlier, and nothing seemed to be moving below me, nothing large enough to leave a track through new-fallen snow. The landscape was nearly as still from the highway. Snowmobiles had run along the ditches, and steers had in some places been turned out into the cornfields, but those were the only signs of movement.

Except for the wind. One family on a farm outside Clara City had put a life-sized Santa Claus on a telephone pole, arms and legs wrapped around it as though Santa were hanging on to keep the prevailing wind from blowing him away like so much topsoil. It was no exaggeration. On the farm I had come to visit, we walked between the house and the sow barn with all the haste we could muster, heads bowed, talking only in the lee. The temperature had already fallen twenty degrees that day, and it was still going down, dropping as fast, it seemed, as the second hand on its way toward six.

I was supposed to return to that farm for supper. I left the motel in the early darkness and headed west out of Willmar, in Kandiyohi County. The wind had risen even higher and was now on its hind legs, a steady gale out of the northwest, and with the rising wind the snow rose too. Sometimes I could see the sulfur glow of lights on a turkey barn or the double halo of approaching headlights. Then the snow thickened, and the highway disappeared into the nullifying glare of my own headlights. Six miles outside of town, in an unbroken whiteout, I turned around.

It was the first time I ever felt the vertigo that settlers often felt when they first came to the prairie. There are many descriptions of it, but here's what I understood. When the wind blows from the northwest in western Minnesota, it blows from infinity. Northwest is the one direction that goes on forever there, without any barriers, beyond the indiscernible horizon and away to the arctic. Most of the fence lines are gone in that cash-grain country, and there's no such thing as a tree line, no rimrock or buttes to hold in the landscape. There's only the sound of the wind skirling down with its endless driven snows upon you.

＊ ＝◊＝ ＊

The snow that fell at home this past weekend was a predatory snow, heavy, wet, and punishing. It fell hastily, clumsily, and by the time the storm ended, there was as much precipitation stacked overhead in the tangled woods, waiting to precipitate, as there was on the ground. It looked as though someone had turned up the planet's gravity during the night. Under the weight of the snow, every tree, every bush, every wire in sight, bowed closer to the earth than it did the day before. Dead limbs snapped under the strain and so did live ones.

The day after the storm — Sunday — was clear and warm, but snow continued to fall. The sun probed the woods, and limb by limb, twig by twig, the tree crowns began to shed their burdens. The conifers whose boughs cant downward naturally emptied themselves first, and then, as the wind began to stir, the rest of the trees joined in. The falling snow sounded like an intermittent rain of small rodents falling on the skylights. Out in the woods the dull concussion of wet snow landing in wet snow was audible everywhere, accompanied by the groan of a black birch or a red maple and the sound of snowmelt running downstream. Every clod that fell from overhead trailed behind it a column of snowflakes hesitating in the sun. For a while, near noon, the air seemed overcharged with brightness.

But by evening the comfortable gloom of December had returned. Nearly all the snow in the treetops had slipped away, and with it the illusion that daylight had somehow been trapped in the canopy above. The woods had reerected themselves. Sunset came and went, and all the color in the natural landscape drained away with it. Blue Christmas bulbs strung along the gables of an old farmhouse, or the orange glow of an incandescent lamp seen through a roadside window at twilight, made it plain how utterly the world had been reduced to black and white. The cold came on a little deeper that night, and in the morning the snow on the woodpile was spiked with frost.

Last week a tree farmer told me there was only an inch of frost in the ground, which was true when he said it. Now there's more, and I've set aside plans to dig a hole for the blue spruce I was buying. But I was struck by the common expression — frost in the ground. It sounds so porous somehow, a web of crystals latticing their way down through the snow and the sod, in among the Japanese beetle grubs lying in wait for next summer. After bitter nights and a steady hard wind these past few days, the panes in the windows have been covered with frost. When the sun strikes those windows, the frost melts instantly and the meltwater evaporates almost as quickly, leaving behind dust prints where there had been drops. It all seems so fragile, so nineteenth century.

But there's nothing porous or fragile or antiquated about frost in the ground. It's the brutalism of winter, a stern, domineering, eyeless fact. The blowing snow seems harsh, as unforgiving and protean as the wind that drives it. Every morning there are new contours of overnight drifting, cornices arcing outward from stone outcrops, hollows at the base of trees, unexpected depths on the smooth downslope of a hillside. Even the sound of the snow underfoot changes from hour to hour. But in the barnyard, a week of horse traffic has barely knocked the peaks off the mud ridges that formed when the last hard freeze came. People often compare frost in the ground to iron or steel, but those tend to be people who have never tried to dig a grave for a dog with a six-foot pry bar in mid-January, as I once did at the pleading of a mournful friend. Frost feels harder than iron or steel. Not even death is as hard as frost in the ground.

When the frost retreats come spring, in a warm rain or under a hot sun, it will retreat with a load of subterranean stone in its grasp, creating a thin, horizontal moraine across the pasture, and yet it will leave the beetle grubs where they lie. But there's almost nothing you can't make use of if you put your mind to it, and that includes frost. In late February or early March, when the snow has melted but the ground is still frozen, I'm going to scatter a mix of red clover and bird's-foot trefoil seed over the pasture. This is called frost seeding.

It sounds like a way to sow ice crystals, or a version of the biblical proverb about seed falling on stony ground. But as the frost relents, the ground expands and contracts and expands again, and the seeds will work their way down into the soil, where they germinate. It's an old idea, as old as the weeds along the tree line. Even now the snow is flecked with hundreds of thousands — perhaps millions — of weed seeds, all waiting for that slow melting ride down to the ground.

The horses have strewn a green carpet of hay underfoot, and two crows feed at its edge. The snow has buried nearly everything in that pasture, but what it hasn't buried it has thrown into silhouette. The tops of the tallest grasses and weeds protrude from the whiteness. On sharp days when there has been light wind and a new inch or two, the weed stems cut a V in the snow. When the wind has been especially strong, the weed tops — their inflorescences — leave a distinctive print, a brushmark, on the surface.

An abandoned clearing that was full of color in August or June now displays the remnants of only a few plants, stiff, skeletal forms still bearing seed against the spring. The blankness of the background confers a kind of unaccustomed grandeur on some of the plants that still stand upright. Burdocks — most grasping, most contemptible of weeds — spread like ancient oaks. Galls appear like minarets high on a clump of weed stalks. Goldenrods bend as though they were seaweed swayed by a light current. The ingenuity, the evolutionary virtuosity, of botanical design becomes apparent among the motherwort, a plant with carillon after carillon of empty, spiny bells surrounding its four-sided stalk.

In late December I feel an almost painful hunger for light. The open woods, bereft of leaves, and the snow itself feel like a kind of appeasement, a way of making amends to my eye for the almost grudging tread of the sun across the sky. That hunger is what makes the detail of the natural world so precious now. Pale green lichen on a tree trunk has all the power of a daylily in bloom. Where moss insulates a south-facing rock outcrop, a few ferns remain May green. The color, like the very plushness of the moss, seems almost inconceivable.

It's tempting to think of winter as the negation of life, but life has too many sequences, too many rhythms, to be altogether quieted by snow and cold. Why are there still leaves on the maple boughs that snapped off in a big storm this autumn? How does it happen that midges hatch on a day just slightly warmer than the rest of the week? They rise from the brook and follow its course upstream, into the darkness of a hemlock wood.

—+— ≡♦≡ —+—

At our place the horses don't eat from mangers. They gather at feeding time in a corner of the pasture near the water tank and the run-in shed, and they take their grain from heavy rubber pans set on the ground. When the horses finish their oats, they toss the hay out of the feeder and paw the flakes apart, as if they were searching for something in the smell of dried grass. Sometimes at this time of year it's hard to tell in the rain and fog where the darkness of day ends and the darkness of night begins. Mud clings to hooves and boots, and it dries on the horses' flanks. Now at last the mud has frozen, making the footing better for everyone. It's been possible once again to see stars at night and to watch, at feeding time, the sky dying out in the pale rose of winter.

The manger in which — the story reads — that infant lay so long ago, whose manger was it? Its wood was smoothed, as if in preparation, by the tongues of animals. In a manger where oats or corn are fed, the softer wood erodes in time and the wood grain appears to rise, glistening when a cow has just done eating and the planks are still wet. In a manger full of hay, a horse will often begin to feed at the very center, shaping a hollow, a nest, of grass or alfalfa. But in paintings of the Nativity, the manger has always been consecrated to another need, and the animals have been displaced, uncomplaining, from their meal. By the time the Wise Men come from Herod — so again say all the paintings — the manger has reverted to its proper use. The beasts are nose-deep in their fodder, but they look up, enfolding Magi, mother, and infant in a world where chores are meant to be done, the animals fed, at the same time every day no matter who comes to visit.

There were eyes that would have been hard to gaze upon that Christmas Eve and Christmas morning many years ago. Fear is what the shepherds felt when the good news was announced. But in the eyes of their flock and in the eyes of the ox and ass depicted in every Nativity, there's the implacable mildness seen even now among the horses when the sun finally warms them. They lie down in the pasture, in the snow, their legs folded beneath them, and steam begins to rise from their sorrel and bay and rose-gray backs. Their repose is a sign of confidence, of safety, and it washes over the person who gets to bring them their hay, which they accept, every morning, as if every morning were Christmas.

December

⊶ ⊷ ⊶ ⊷ ⊶

The next-to-last leg of a long day was the flight from Denver into Casper, Wyoming, and touchdown just at sunset. That flight restored everything to scale — a slow turboprop plane, more than half empty, the Casper airport, nearly deserted except for a man and woman in National Guard uniforms with black rifles slung barrel down across their backs. I sat behind the wing, looking out at the rivets on the trailing edge. The snow-matted thatch of Colorado hovered below, the corridor of tilled and irrigated ground running north from Denver to Fort Collins and breaking suddenly in the country near the Wyoming line, where an ocean of short grass spread without interruption to the dark eastern horizon.

I'd spent all day in crowds, at check-in counters, in security lines, in the thigh and elbow crush of viewless airliners. And now, here at last, coming into Wyoming, was the pure impassioned abstraction of flying once again, the ground subsiding at takeoff, the occasional sideways skid of the plane on the currents of air, the shuddering and ticking as crosswinds caught us on the final approach. It felt like a right recovered, a perspective too vital to be curtailed. Long wind-shadows, cast by haystacks and windbreaks, stretched eastward across the snowy plains. The eastern furrows still held snow in the great center-pivot circles of irrigated ground, though the western furrows had blown dry. The sinuous trackings of runoff creeks looked like the insect runes you sometimes see carved just beneath the bark on a round of firewood. The ranch buildings below had herded together out of the cold wind, into the pale reach of a yardlight.

The last leg was by car in darkness down the long stretch of blacktop that passes westward through Powder River, Moneta, Shoshoni, and on into Riverton. Snow had piled up along the edges of a railroad shed and in eroded hollows out of the wind, but elsewhere the snow shone mostly like a version of the moon's thin light. A coyote stood beside the highway, his coat brush-thick, looking like a crossing guard with miles and miles of crossings to watch over. The Powder River sign, population 50, seemed to be exaggerating. Eastbound trucks slung past in the opposite lane, traveling within a self-propelled storm of grit. Cattle had begun to bed down along the fence lines where hay had been fed.

A winter night can seem almost infinite here under the smooth, cold sky. The last of the day's heat in the blacktop and the bare fortifications of rock has long since drifted away. Even the smallest undulations in the open ground, the tightest switches of grass, look like welcome cover from a wind that, in imagination at least, is always blowing. When you near a town like Lander, the sense of relief comes not so much from the streetlights, which are hidden until the very last, but from the depth of the hills, from the willows that encroach on the rivers and creeks, from a gray coppiced look that promises shelter. The cottonwoods in town have that look too, a witch's head of bare, tangled branches against the night. The streets lie still and broad, the houses lit within themselves, the darkness deep and even.

December

❧ ⚜ ❧

I wake up sometimes at night, two or three o'clock, and walk to a window that looks out over the pasture. Some nights the moon is high in its December arc, so different from the angle it cuts through the sky in summer. Its light falls like a pale shadow among the white birches on the hillside. But on nights when the sky is hidden by clouds, when I can almost feel my pupils dilating in the search for a reference point outdoors, I turn to a flat panel of light that shines out along the fence line. It comes from a bulb in the chicken house that clicks on automatically at one-thirty in the morning. Dawn comes abruptly to the chickens. I imagine them blinking at reveille on their roosts.

The light is a trick, a way of fooling the hens into thinking that summer lingers on and that laying time is still here. Our hens are young. Until December 22 they had never laid an egg. But on the day after the winter solstice, in time with the returning sun, we found a brown pullet egg, still warm, in the hay below the nest boxes. It was an occasion of great mutual satisfaction. The roosters, still far too numerous and a pox on each other's contentment, didn't notice the event at all. Until you've watched roosters chase each other round and round, propelled by their hormones, you have no idea how much they can move like Groucho Marx. They're that sardonic too.

Only a few weeks ago the roosters were young enough to be called cockerels, their voices still breaking. One by one they tried to crow as they lounged around the chicken yard, but the

crowing always sounded as though Reynard the Fox had a paw
on their throats, or as though they were using a straight mute in
their trumpets. Now they sing out loud and clear, in different
pitches, with widely differing takes on the canonical cock-a-
doodle-doo. Why there should be so much pleasure in listening
to the crowing of a rooster who really knows his business I don't
understand. I sometimes imagine the sound the sun would
make if we could hear it coming up. I think of that sound as a
great processional march — the musical movement of Sol's
robes over the eastern sky — but not so grand that there wasn't
a note of hilarity in it. The hilarity is provided by a crowing
rooster.

Watching these chickens grow, building a house for them,
getting to understand how they regard the world, I've been surprised again and again by how much of what I know about
chickens comes from the cartoons I watched as a kid. Not that I
expected the senatorial presence of Foghorn Leghorn in our
Buff Orpington roosters or the opulent, Odalisque-like preen-
ing of cartoon hens. But I recognize the incessant barnyard
drama from the cartoons, and when my dad and I built the
chicken house in October I couldn't resist adding a slatted ramp
of the kind that every cartoon chicken house always had. Now
when I get up in the middle of the night and see the chicken
light burning, throwing a yellow glow out into the darkness, I
find myself comforted and go back to bed and to sleep.

To the Reader

The notes and observations in *The Rural Life* were written over several years, but they've been gathered together in these pages into a single calendar year. If spring seems to be well advanced on one page but balky and weeks behind on the next, you can blame it on the weather or on the fact that I'm probably describing two very different springs. I hope the occasional sudden shifts in the seasons of this book are no more erratic than what the weather actually brings us these days.

Most of these brief essays were published in a different form on the editorial page of the *New York Times*, under the rubric "The Rural Life." Others appeared in *The New Yorker*, *GQ*, *This Old House*, and *DoubleTake*. I'm indebted to Howell Raines, Gail Collins, and my colleagues on the *Times* editorial board. For their considerable editorial contributions along the way, I'd also like to thank Bob Gottlieb, Chip McGrath, Ilena Silverman, Dave Grogan, Steve Petranek, and Albert LaFarge. I owe special thanks, as always, to my agent, Flip Brophy.

The Rural Life could not have been written without the daily help and inspiration of my wife and partner in rural living, Lindy Smith. She knows better than anyone how much this book belongs to her.

About the Author

VERLYN KLINKENBORG was born in Colorado and raised in Iowa and California. He graduated from Pomona College and received a Ph.D. in English Literature from Princeton University. He is the author of *Making Hay* and *The Last Fine Time*, and his work has also appeared in many magazines. Since 1997 he has been a member of the editorial board of the *New York Times*. He lives in rural New York state with his wife, the photographer Lindy Smith.

A Note on the Type

This book was set in a digitized version of Baskerville, based on the typeface designed by typefounder and printer John Baskerville in 1752. By the mid–eighteenth century, printing, paper, and typography standards had reached an all-time low. Baskerville dramatically upgraded the craft of all three, producing beautiful volumes, including John Milton's *Paradise Lost* in 1758, and Baskerville's much-acclaimed masterpiece, the Cambridge University Bible, in 1763. Baskerville typefaces are still much admired for their beautiful proportions and extreme legibility, making them well suited for both book design and advertising.